NOTRE DAME
CATHEDRAL

NOTRE DAME
CATHEDRAL
Nine Centuries of History

Dany Sandron and Andrew Tallon
Translated by Lindsay Cook and Andrew Tallon

The Pennsylvania State University Press | University Park, Pennsylvania

Library of Congress Cataloging-in-Publication Data

Names: Sandron, Dany, author. | Tallon, Andrew, 1969–2018, author. |
    Cook, Lindsay (Lindsay Shepherd), translator.
Title: Notre-Dame of Paris : nine centuries of history / written by
    Dany Sandron and Andrew Tallon ; translated by Lindsay Cook.
Other titles: Notre-Dame de Paris. English
Description: University Park, Pennsylvania : The Pennsylvania State
    University Press, [2020] | Includes bibliographical references
    and index. | Summary: "A visual survey of the cathedral of
    Notre Dame in Paris over the past 850 years. Addresses a
    series of key themes in the cathedral's history, including the
    fundraising campaign, the construction of vaults, and the
    liturgical function of the choir"—Provided by publisher.
Identifiers: LCCN 2019040791 | ISBN 9780271086224 (paperback)
Subjects: LCSH: Notre-Dame de Paris (Cathedral)—History. | Church
    architecture—France—Paris—History. | Architecture, Gothic—
    France—Paris. | Church decoration and ornament—France—
    Paris—History. | Paris (France)—Buildings, structures, etc.
Classification: LCC NA5550.N7 S2613 2020 | DDC
    726.50944/361—dc23
LC record available at https://lccn.loc.gov/2019040791

Notre-Dame de Paris: Neuf siècles d'histoire
Dany Sandron / Andrew Tallon
Copyright © Editions Parigramme, 2013 Paris, France

English translation © The Pennsylvania State University
All rights reserved
Printed in Turkey
Published by The Pennsylvania State University Press,
University Park, PA 16802–1003

The Pennsylvania State University Press is a member of the
Association of University Presses.

It is the policy of The Pennsylvania State University Press to use
acid-free paper. Publications on uncoated stock satisfy the minimum
requirements of American National Standard for Information
Sciences—Permanence of Paper for Printed Library Material,
ANSI z39.48–1992.

*Published in memory of Andrew Tallon (1969–2018),
who gave so much to Notre Dame and whose work
will guide its future restoration.*

CONTENTS

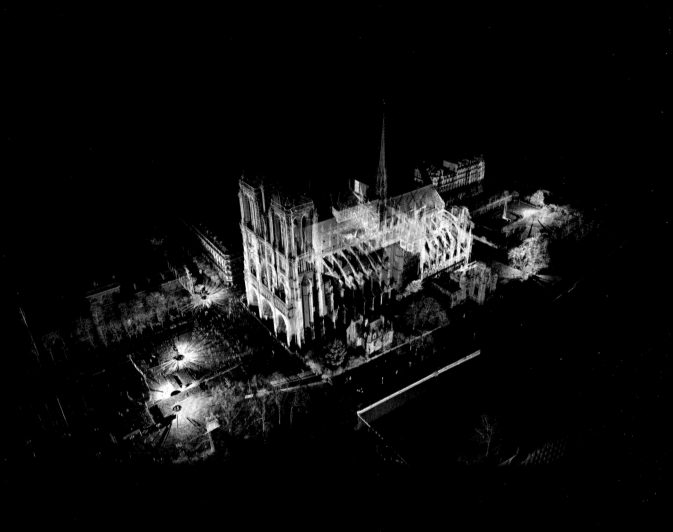

1. Laser survey of Notre Dame

Introduction

Notre Dame in Paris is the Gothic cathedral par excellence. It had an immediate impact because its architecture represented a challenge in the second half of the twelfth century. Perhaps this is hardly surprising, given its ties to people in high places and its geographic location in the heart of a city that was fully becoming the capital of the kingdom of France.

The construction of an edifice as immense as Notre Dame came at a high point for the episcopacy in the history of the Church. Bishop Maurice de Sully, who launched the campaign, exemplified the ideal prelate of the period: at once an eminent intellectual and an effective administrator. He ably coordinated the efforts within the diocese he oversaw to have a bold monument constructed; the project reflected the clergy's ambition to blend in with all levels of society to realize its essential mission as spiritual guide to a society for whose salvation it was responsible.

In Paris, the situation was unique due to the proximity, both literal and figurative, of the king. From his palace situated at the opposite end of the Île de la Cité, the sovereign could easily visit Notre Dame. In a society in which ritual played a crucial role, Notre Dame was the site of important royal ceremonies: during his first entrance into Paris, even before going to his own palace, the king would go to Notre Dame to confirm his protection of the cathedral clergy. It was also in the cathedral of Paris that a wake would take place the night before a royal burial. As such, Notre Dame shared with the cathedral of Reims (the royal coronation church) and the abbey church of Saint-Denis (the royal necropolis) the status of sanctuaries favored by the monarchy.

Contemporaneous events attest, however laconically, to the cathedral's construction. In 1179, in the great hall of the episcopal palace, Prince Philip—the future King Philip II Augustus—was designated the successor to his father, Louis VII, at that point gravely ill, by acclamation of the important figures in the kingdom. As early as 1190, it was in the new choir that Philip's wife, Queen Isabelle of Hainaut, was buried. Joining her in 1218 was the young prince Philip, the eldest son of Louis VIII and Blanche of Castile, leaving the throne open for his younger brother Louis IX (r. 1226–70). The closeness of the Church of Paris to the Capetian monarchy affected the functioning of both institutions: the Parisian clergy was often solicited to counsel the royal government, and the sovereign intervened frequently in the operations of the Church. In 1302, Philip IV (Philip the Fair) brought together a large assembly to support him politically when confronted with a critical papacy: this event has sometimes been framed as the first general assembly in French history, and it was at the very least a strong symbol of the close connection between the cathedral clergy and the monarchy. This symbiosis was maintained from one generation to another, despite certain intervening events, such as the foundation of the Sainte-Chapelle, which, situated a few steps from Notre Dame, became the chief repository in the realm for relics with the acquisition by Louis IX of the relics of the Passion of Christ in 1239 and 1241. That five centuries later Louis XIII would make Notre Dame the sanctuary where he vowed to place the kingdom under the protection of the Virgin Mary says a great deal about the lasting bond between inextricably linked political and ecclesiastical powers.

Notre Dame enjoyed royal privileges under successive regimes, always linked to the dignity that the cathedral impressed upon the events to which political forces wished to give a national flavor—from the consecration of Napoleon to the funerals of heads of state, from diplomatic visits to important moments in the country's history.

Notre Dame's privileged link, since the twelfth century, to the political apparatus also explains the success its architecture and decorative program have since enjoyed. The diffusion of both throughout the Christian world and beyond evidently benefitted from this connection. The gallery of kings crowning the three western portals of the façade, with its twenty-eight colossal statues, became the prototype for a vast number of similar compositions elsewhere. The gallery of Reims (centered on the baptism of Clovis, a founding event of the French monarchy and its close relationship to the Church), that of the cathedral of Burgos with the kings of Castile, and the equestrian statues of the façade of Strasbourg celebrating the protective sovereigns of the area are all proof of the success of the Parisian invention.

Even if taller, more ornamented, or bolder edifices were constructed later on, in Paris and beyond, the cathedral became a point of reference, thanks to a series of innovations that placed it in the avant-garde of the architecture of its day. It played a determining role from the beginning of the modern reception of Gothic architecture. The way the edifice harnessed space astounded architects and aesthetes of the Enlightenment, who were as fascinated by its structural audacity as they were inclined to reject that which had, in their view, spoiled the ensemble: the indecipherable sculptures attached to its façades.

Left abandoned for forty years following the French Revolution, at the dawn of the nineteenth century, through the works of illustrious writers like Chateaubriand and Hugo, the cathedral became the keystone of a nascent movement that attempted to give medieval cultural heritage its rightful place in French history. Transformed into a gigantic laboratory where the architects Jean-Baptiste Lassus and Eugène Viollet-le-Duc could dissect, dismantle, put back, and reconstruct whatever elements they wished, the monument found itself at the center of progress in the realm of restoration practice. Their interventions became the subject of precise scientific reports in many publications, chief among them the *Dictionnaire* of Viollet-le-Duc.

The art historian Marcel Aubert was the first to attempt to untangle the complex history, historiography, and archaeology of the edifice, producing a viable synthesis in 1909. It was, for all intents and purposes, a monograph, despite his reluctance to use the term, perhaps knowing that he would not have the last word on the subject. Over the course of the twentieth century, specialists, in turn, became interested in this canonical monument, with perhaps less enthusiasm than they exhibited for other Gothic buildings. If ink continued to be spilled, arguments were advanced with less conviction (and often little more than hypotheses): the accepted wisdom was that the vast restoration campaign undertaken in the nineteenth century irremediably compromised all archaeological study of the medieval edifice.

In our own day, Notre Dame appears as the building that has attracted the most poetry, the most prose, in short, more words than any other: a monument of words erected in honor of this emblematic monument of stone. Notre Dame, "memorial of France," to borrow a phrase from Pierre du Colombier, is visited each year by more than fourteen million visitors, a number far exceeding the several hundred thousand faithful who frequented the cathedral in the Middle Ages, primarily on important feast days. Swallowed up by the crowd, it is difficult to grasp the complexity of the edifice, retrofitted constantly over the centuries.

From this point of view, 3-D modeling offers fresh perspectives. At the core of this book is a 3-D laser scan realized in January 2010 **(fig. 1)**; composed of over a billion data points, with a margin of error of less than 5 millimeters, the laser survey furnished an extremely accurate spatial map of the building, itself dissected and reconstructed—virtually, thanks to the skill of Laurence Stefanon—in order to tell the story through images of the construction and reconstruction of Notre Dame over the past 850 years.

The 3-D model makes explicit to the nonspecialist and expert alike both the structure and massing of the great church: it enables us not only to inspect the edifice closely, down to the last detail, but also to immerse ourselves fully in the monument even better than if we were there in person. The historical dimension is made tangible by hypothetical reconstructions of important moments in the construction, retrofitting, and restoration of the building. The cathedral is the product of a long history, set in motion by a building campaign that was far from linear, from the 1160s until the middle of the thirteenth century. The considerable changes undertaken up to the mid-fourteenth century transformed it into the archetypal Gothic church, fitted with immense windows made possible by the sophisticated system of skeletal flying buttresses. It is this image that persists today, countered or exacerbated by later interventions that have made it for the past 150 years one of the paragons of restoration history and an essential example of world heritage.

Regardless of the angle from which we choose to view the cathedral, a picture is worth a thousand words, or at least it has the capacity to communicate a massive amount of information acquired over the centuries. More images would be required to exhaust the subject, but the potential of digital imaging makes it possible to go back in time in a cathedral tested by the terrible fire of April 15, 2019, that destroyed its timber framework, lead roof, and spire. The virtual representation here of these lost elements anticipates the careful restoration that will once again give them form. ◆

The Gothic cathedral was preceded by several sanctuaries built and retrofitted from the fourth to the
twelfth century. Next to the great church (perhaps
already dedicated to Notre Dame) and reconstructed
here in a very hypothetical manner were located,
from west to east, the church of Saint Christopher,
the centrally planned baptistery of Saint John, and
three churches parallel to one another in front of
Saint-Denis-du-Pas.

1163

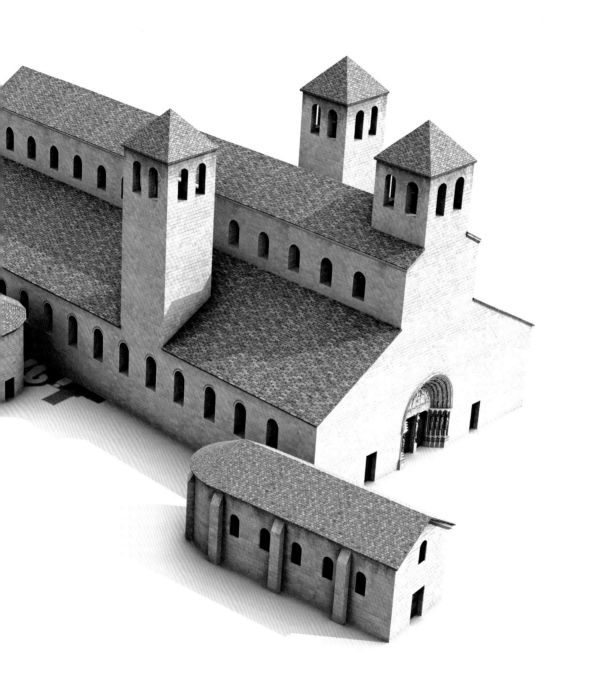

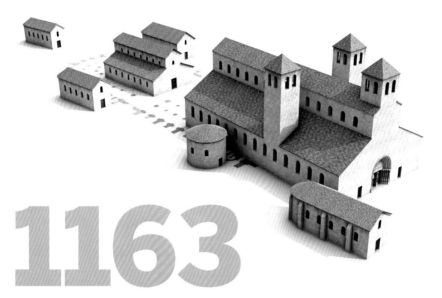

1163

Planning the Cathedral

Beginning in the 1160s, the Gothic cathedral progressively replaced several earlier buildings, many of them relatively small in scale, situated at the east end of the Île de la Cité. Often in a precarious state of preservation, these diverse edifices offered a glimpse of the long history of the mother church of the diocese, which dated back to the fourth century.

The written sources attest to the existence of three sanctuaries at the beginning of the twelfth century, including a church dedicated to Saint Stephen—perhaps from the Early Middle Ages—and another dedicated to the Virgin Mary, attested from the ninth century. None of them may be firmly localized. To those mentioned above should be added the church

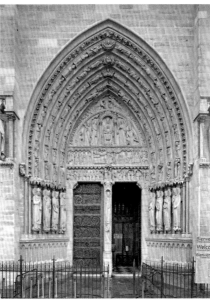

of Saint-Jean-le-Rond—whose dedication retained the memory of an earlier baptistery with a centralized plan—and the church of Saint-Denis-du-Pas, both of which, after being rebuilt, remained standing until the eighteenth century, the former immediately to the north of the west façade of the Gothic cathedral and the latter next to its chevet.

   Archaeological finds excavated since the eighteenth century at various sites within the cathedral precinct have led to the recovery of some vestiges of these edifices, without settling the vexing question of their construction chronology or the numerous transformations they underwent. It is likely that the situation in the Early Middle Ages was characterized by the existence of at least two sanctuaries. The façade of the largest edifice, which had as many as five aisles, was situated a few dozen meters to the west of the portals of the existing Gothic building. It was perhaps for this edifice that a large portal dedicated to the Virgin Mary was created in the mid-twelfth century **(fig. 1)**, whose main features (tympanum, jamb-figures, and archivolts carved with figural sculpture) were reused at the beginning of the thirteenth century in the Saint Anne portal, on the south side of the west façade **(fig. 2)**. This monumental decoration fit in well with the dimensions of the cathedral, 70 meters in length, an imposing structure with respect to the sanctuaries situated to the east, which were significantly smaller in scale and beginning to show signs of their age.

1163

Planning the Cathedral

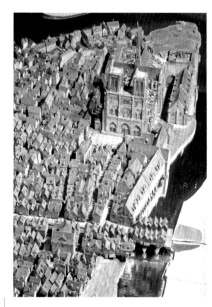

3. The construction of a new cathedral was the most visible element of a vast urban reconfiguration, which likewise included the reconstruction of the episcopal palace and the transfer of the Hôtel-Dieu to the bank of the short branch of the Seine. This late nineteenth-century model depicts the Île de la Cité as it looked in the late Middle Ages (Musée Carnavalet).

The desire to design a more fitting venue for the liturgy, a place that could accommodate even great numbers of the faithful, and a symbol that would project the power of the institution with respect to others in the city and throughout the diocese led the cathedral clergy to launch, around the year 1160, an extraordinary building project that would completely transform the heart of the city.

Responsibility for overseeing construction naturally fell to the bishop and the cathedral chapter. The clergy defined the parameters of the new edifice to respond to specific needs. They were also responsible for raising the funds necessary to finance the project, acquiring the raw materials, and recruiting and paying the workers. A new institution known as the cathedral fabric, an offshoot of the cathedral chapter, managed these accounts. The cathedral chapter always played an important role in overseeing construction.

The Bishop

In a world in which power was extremely personalized, it was the bishop, the leader of the diocese—a geographic region corresponding, more or less, to the Paris region—who was at the forefront of the history of the construction of the cathedral. It was beyond a shadow of a doubt Maurice de Sully, bishop from 1160 to 1196, who had the idea to construct a new church that would surpass all previous monuments in magnitude. The bishop invested all his energy in this project: in overseeing the goods and property of the bishopric, he increased revenue and may have invested part of it in the construction project; in his role as a preacher, he solicited offerings from the faithful, many of whom supported this project; and he himself donated funds of his own. Not content solely with launching a campaign

4. Transferred to the ambulatory, the tomb effigy of Bishop Simon de Bucy originated in the axial chapel he founded in 1296 to house his grave.

for a new cathedral, he also had the bishop's palace built to the south of the cathedral, and once the area surrounding the future façade was cleared, he had the Hôtel-Dieu transferred all the way to the bank of the Seine **(fig. 3)**. It amounted to a veritable urbanism effort, the likes of which medieval Paris had rarely seen. The bishop's successors took up the baton: as such, Eudes de Sully (1196–1208), during whose episcopacy the façade was begun, enacted synodal statutes regulating the clergy throughout the diocese. He also stipulated that the faithful should visit the cathedral, the mother church, at least once a year. Later on, Guillaume de Seignelay (1219–24) insisted that priests solicit participation from the laity to finance the cathedral, and Guillaume d'Auvergne (1228–49) donated the largest bell to the cathedral, which was placed in the north tower and named after the bishop. Late thirteenth- and early fourteenth-century bishops carried on the effort, having cathedral furnishings renewed and new chapels built, including the axial chapel, which the founding bishop Simon de Bucy (d. 1304) chose as his final resting place **(fig. 4)**. His stone tomb and painted effigy located against one of the chapel walls stamped the east end of the cathedral with the episcopal imprint, at the opposite end of the building from the façade whose south portal highlighted some of his prestigious predecessors: Saint Marcel in the trumeau (the original is in the Musée de Cluny) and, opposite a kneeling king, a prelate standing near the Virgin Mary in the tympanum **(fig. 5)**.

5. In the Saint Anne portal, the twelfth-century depiction of a bishop of Paris assisted by a scribe celebrates episcopal power.

6. Master of Dunois, *Throne of Grace and Canons of Notre-Dame*, mid-fifteenth century (Paris, ENSBA). Initially destined to decorate the altar of the Trinity (at the end of the apse), the retable features the cathedral's college of canons.

The Cathedral Chapter

To assist the bishop in the exercise of his duties and offer him counsel, a group of clerics was assembled in the ninth century to form a chapter of canons. At the end of the twelfth century, this community had fifty-one members **(fig. 6)**. They bore the responsibility of electing the bishop. Dignitaries of the chapter exercised extraordinary authority: the dean had power over the entire community, and the cantor was responsible not only for chant but in fact for all aspects of the liturgy that determined aspects of the services and ceremonies that took place in the cathedral choir. Peter the Chanter, who held the office of cantor at the end of the twelfth century, was a notable moralizing figure within the institution of the Church of Paris, whose inclination toward excess and architectural superfluity he criticized, albeit in vain. This particularly critical position remained an isolated event, and the canons generally favored spectacular building projects, as evidenced by the successive additions to the cathedral. The communal structure of the cathedral chapter ensured continuity, and over the course of construction, its role became more prominent.

The presence of a seated cleric, probably a canon, depicted in the process of writing on the left side of the tympanum of the Saint Anne portal (south portal of the west façade) may allude to the important role the cathedral chapter played in the life of the diocese.

The Fabric

The term "fabric" was used to designate the institution charged with managing the funds dedicated to the construction and maintenance of the cathedral. From the twelfth century, it was part of one of the principal offices of the cathedral chapter: the chamber of the chapter. Its administrator was a canon, bearing the title

1163

Planning the Cathedral

7. Effigy of Canon Pierre de Fayel, from the choir screen, before 1344 (Louvre, département des Sculptures, LP 540).

of chamberlain, who was responsible for administering funds, either alone or with another delegate. A charter of 1123 specifies that some of these responsibilities fell to the canon responsible for the chevet (*chevecier*) and another canon chosen by both chapter and bishop: the two, in their role as guardians (*custodes*), were responsible for its management. The canon responsible for the chevet had control over the offerings of the faithful, a significant revenue stream.

Thus, this body oversaw the collection and distribution of funds. The substantial sums amassed explain why both bishop and chapter exerted strict control over them.

Resources

It is impossible to evaluate the total construction cost of Notre Dame, since no account books survive from any part of the project, but it likely cost hundreds of thousands of livres, a colossal sum at the time. The intervention of a single person, no matter how wealthy, would not suffice to carry out an enterprise encompassing the architecture, sculpture, and furnishings. In canon law, a

fourth of the property of each church was intended for the upkeep and repair of religious edifices. This amount could come from the clergy's revenue, from the bishop's *mense* and the canons' *mense*—that is, the property of the bishop and chapter, respectively—or from lay donations. Donations could be made in cash or in kind. The latter consisted of property from which revenue would flow to the fabric, sumptuous objects that could enrich the treasury or be traded to cover costs, or even beasts of burden to pull the carts filled with construction materials.

The clergy, impacted directly by the building enterprise, did not neglect to supply it with funds, both collective and individual, which their great wealth made possible. Their role seems even greater than the details

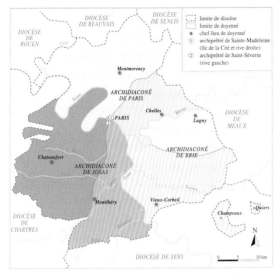

8. Map of the former configuration of the diocese of Paris.

scrupulously maintained in their own archives (the principal surviving evidence of the financing of the project) would suggest.

Episcopal Donations

There are numerous references to episcopal donations, beginning with the initiating bishop, Maurice de Sully. Contemporary chroniclers emphasized the fact that he used for the cathedral less the gifts of others than the revenues associated with his office as bishop. His gifts as an administrator, which made Louis VII favor his election as bishop in 1160, were a sight to behold: he assembled effective teams who oversaw the agricultural land and residential property associated with the institution he led, which largely facilitated the fundraising for the building campaign. He himself also donated 100 livres to the fabric for the cathedral's lead roof, an amount equivalent at that time to the price of a house

on the Île de la Cité. His example inspired his successors Renaud de Corbeil (1268) and Simon de Bucy (1304), who donated equivalent sums.

Capitular Donations

Due to its wealth and its direct involvement in the building project, the cathedral chapter actively financed the cathedral's construction.

The necrology of the chapter, which records the names of departed patrons of the cathedral for whom anniversary masses were celebrated, records multiple individual donations made by its members. Among the oldest, from the last third of the twelfth century, are those of Dean Barbedor, who donated a stained-glass window worth 15 livres to the fabric of Notre Dame, and the cantor Albert, who gave 20 livres for the construction of the choir stalls. The bequest of the canon Raymond de Clermont of more than 1,000 livres was, in part, diverted from its original purpose in order to remake the shrine of Saint Marcel in the 1260s. Many canons distinguished themselves by founding private chapels, such as Girard de Courlandon, who had the chapel of Saint Nicaise built in the chevet. The canon Pierre de Fayel (d. 1344) had himself depicted praying near his place of burial, in the ambulatory behind the axial bay of the choir, on a portion of the choir screen he, in part, financed **(fig. 7)**.

Lay Donations

Lay offerings constituted a significant revenue source: they resulted from a concerted fundraising effort undertaken throughout the diocese **(fig. 8)**, the progress of which the bishop tracked at diocesan synods. Guillaume de Seignelay took care to insist that priests solicit

1163

Planning the Cathedral

donations from their flocks, even threatening them with sanctions if they did not comply. The sermons of itinerant preachers likewise encouraged the laity to support the campaign. To these should be added offerings made on site at altars, in kind or in cash; offerings left in the relic box (dedicated to Saint Denis in an act of 1190); and, finally, extraordinary offerings at the altar, placed on the veil known as the succinctorium, which was used to dress the altar on certain solemn feast days.

In the early thirteenth century, the legate Eudes de Châteauroux specified that these donations, often major, were largely made by women, whose generosity he acknowledged: "There is no shrewd merchant who would turn down a small offering. It was with small donations from women that the cathedral of Paris was in large part constructed." While this statement may be slightly exaggerated, it seems to hold water. Another author of the thirteenth century, Thomas de Cobham,

documented the custom of women offering candles at the altar at Saturday Vespers. This commerce in candles for sale at the doors of the church was so lucrative that members of the clergy vied for control of this market. To encourage donations, bishops could grant indulgences—that is, a remission of sins to those who gave a sum of money for the construction or retrofitting of the cathedral. Maurice de Sully sometimes exercised this power, but he did not abuse it as others did in the late Middle Ages. Even so, reactions suggest that this practice was always somewhat controversial.

Even if these donations were limited in number, we must consider the actions of the kings of France in favor of the cathedral. Louis VII (1137–80) was apparently the most generous, offering 200 livres to the fabric, double the amount Bishop Maurice de Sully is recorded as having given. His son, Philip II Augustus, did not make such lavish donations, but he carried on the paternalistic politics of protecting the Church of Paris. To that end, he committed—although did not always live up to his promise—not to abuse the *droit de régale* or the *droit de dépouille*, royal prerogatives allowing the sovereign to administer the diocese

9 and 10. Once the foundations of the choir were in place, in the 1160s, the construction of the the north side of the choir was begun (the two side aisles and the main arcade of the central vessel) before continuing with the level of the tribunes.

when the episcopal seat was vacant—in order to draw profit from its revenues—and to claim all or part of the personal property of the bishop at his death. On the eve of his departure on crusade, we find Philip Augustus worrying for the future of the construction of the cathedral if by chance Bishop Maurice were to die in the king's absence. In that event, the king dictated that the archbishop of Sens and the cantor of the cathedral of Paris would assume responsibility for the construction project.

The building was truly the result of a collective effort, in the sense that much of the population helped finance its construction, chief among them the inhabitants of the diocese of Paris. Only a community several hundred thousand strong could provide for a building project on the scale of Notre Dame. But there ended the popular input into an enterprise that would require highly skilled labor. To carry out the project, the clergy remained in charge of the operation **(figs. 9 and 10)**. At a time when private investment and public participation were not rigidly separated, a similar dynamism applied to the various means of financing the construction project: individual and institutional donations by the clergy, protection by the powerful, and appeals for lay donations, without scrutinizing the exact source of the funds too closely. ◆

The first two stories of the choir are nearing completion. The platforms are in place for the construction of the third level of the elevation. Note that a series of wooden props were placed at each main pier and against the west-facing walls; these temporary supports were designed to prevent the building from moving as the mortar set.

1170

1170

Building the Cathedral

As we have seen, responsibility for the construction of the cathedral fell to the bishop and chapter. Yet their role was not limited to raising the necessary funds for this major building project: they also coordinated the provisioning of building materials.

Unlike many other contemporaneous Gothic building sites, the bishop and chapter enjoyed a precious resource: namely, the numerous exploitable stone quarries located nearby. In fact, the vast majority of the stone used to construct the cathedral came from sites only a few kilometers away. The same was true of the timber for the roof trusses: it was felled in forests that belonged to the bishop and chapter. As soon as a provisional port

1 and 2. The Notre Dame chevet in 1170 (above) and its 2013 state (below).

was built, the only task that remained was to establish an access route within the dense urban fabric surrounding the old cathedral. This situation was quite different from that of many of the major Gothic building sites—such as Chartres, for example, to which building materials had to be transported considerable distances by cart. When hauling was necessary, notably from the riverbank to the building site, it happened under the best conditions.

In Paris, the transport of construction materials was usually subject to heavy taxes. Acts of 1119 and 1222 exempted those operating carts for the bishop and chapter from paying such taxes.

The Master Mason

We know that Bishop Maurice de Sully was responsible for initiating the project to rebuild the cathedral. And yet the name of the man who envisioned its design—an exceptional vision for a novel edifice unparalleled in its scale and monumentality—remains unknown. Based on surviving documents, the appropriate term for this person is not *architect* but rather *magister*, or "master mason," even though considerable variation exists among the sources: one Richard, called a *cementarius* (mason) in a twelfth-century document related to the cathedral, could just as easily have been the author of the building. On the other hand, this terminological difference is essential: the word "architect" bears a modern connotation that is far from the medieval master mason. Whereas a contemporary architect may be content with designing a building

1170

Building the Cathedral

and providing a series of drawings as guidelines for its construction before moving on to another project, the master mason employed by Maurice de Sully was deeply invested in all aspects of the construction of the cathedral. A specialist in stonemasonry, having learned his craft at other building sites, he was also an expert in carpentry: the challenge of constructing a masonry structure largely depended on the construction of the right scaffolding and formwork for the vaults, crucial for allowing the blocks of stone to be assembled and the mortar to dry. Crucially, the master mason also had to demonstrate a keen organizational sense to complete his task.

The bishop and chapter conveyed their specifications to the master mason: they desired a building that would satisfy the liturgical needs of an expanding episcopate but that would also be able to rival the principal churches in the West. Three monuments, in particular, loomed large: Old Saint Peter's in Rome **(fig. 3)**, the most important church in Christendom; the abbey church of Saint Denis, the architectural pride of the kingdom, whose chevet had just been completed **(fig. 4)**; and the abbey church of Saints Peter and Paul of Cluny, the

abbey church of one of the most powerful monasteries in the world. The master mason was charged with giving shape to the ambitions of the bishop and chapter.

The master mason assimilated these mythic prototypes in four ways. First of all, on the model of Old Saint Peter's and Cluny, Notre Dame was divided into five aisles; second, the cathedral was given a double ambulatory, which had only ever been attempted once before, at Saint-Denis, a short time before; third, columns were selected for the supports of the arcade level, an element directly inspired by early Christian basilicas (likewise a reference to the previous cathedral, demolished to make way for the new); and finally, in a more subtle and unusual way, the flat mural surfaces of the elevation, an essential element of early Christian basilicas, was celebrated at Notre Dame, rejecting the plasticity of the

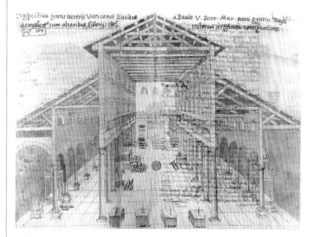

3. Rome, Saint Peter's Basilica, late sixteenth century, section and perspective of the fourth-century basilica that preceded the current church. Giacomo Grimaldi, *Descrizione della basilica antica di S. Pietro in Vaticano* (Rome, Codex Barberini Latin 2733, fols. 104v–105r).

4. Saint-Denis, ambulatory of the abbey church, ca. 1144.

latest architectural styles. And the new cathedral went even further: its height, measured from the pavement to the keystone of the vaults, would equal that of the Constantinian basilica and would surpass the abbey church of Cluny. All this was accomplished in a novel architectural style, which would later be referred to simply as *opus francigenum* ("French work") and which we now call "Gothic."

The master mason was well aware of the flurry of building activity that had marked the previous three decades, whether in the royal domain or in the surrounding regions, where buildings were rebuilt, little by little, in the new architectural style. Surely he knew Sens Cathedral, the seat of the archbishopric, another edifice with a considerable importance in both the political and architectural arenas, as well as the abbey church Saint-Germain-des-Prés, which itself emulated Sens. The master mason drew from a number of rather complex sources: firsthand knowledge of the latest building projects and the enthusiasm palpable in those places, as well as a historicizing vision that sought to glorify the past, exemplified by the choice to configure the space into a five-aisled edifice with columnar supports and flat walls.

The Design

Indeed, the design of the cathedral of Paris may be linked to the plan of Old Saint Peter's in Rome, the

1170

Building the Cathedral

elevation of Cluny, the ambulatory of Saint-Denis, and the vaults of the cathedral of Sens. Still, its construction required its own plan. Such was the principal challenge of a building project: to transform the idea of an edifice, whether a theological or geometrical abstraction, into the stone, mortar, wood, iron, and glass of a physical structure. The plan delineated the entire structure in three dimensions: all of the elements were thus represented, from the foundations to the flying buttresses and from the bays to the vaults.

Based on relatively simple geometrical and arithmetical formulas, the master mason laid out the plan of the chevet on the ground, using wooden stakes and string, according to a unit of measurement known as a perch **(fig. 5)**. The columns and walls were designed around a series of concentric circles: the circle largest in diameter delimited the outermost point of the original

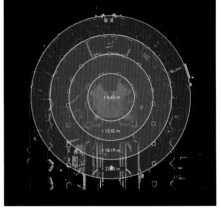

5. Plan of the Notre Dame chevet generated from the laser scan. The underlying elements of the plan were determined by a series of circles with proportional radii, created with the help of ropes of different lengths attached to a stake.

flying buttresses of the choir (subsequently enlarged, as we will see). An equilateral triangle whose base corresponded to the distance from the surface of one outer wall to the other determined the height of the vaults **(fig. 6)**. The entire spatial system of the chevet was conceived in this way.

The master mason of the cathedral of Paris was the first after that of Saint-Denis to dare to design a double ambulatory. Due to the radial arrangement of the supports (and thus their progressive lengthening),

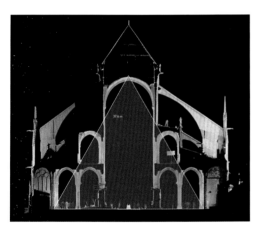

6. Transverse section of the choir generated from the laser scan. An equilateral triangle may be inscribed within the section, indicating that the building's interior width determined the height of the vaults.

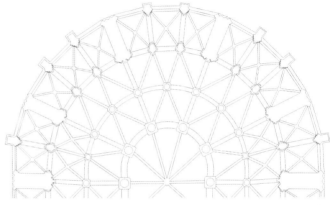

7. Plan of the cathedral's chevet showing the centrifugal arrangement of the piers and the triangular cells of the vaults.

ambulatories were challenging enough to build, but designing a double ambulatory was particularly complex. The master mason came up with an ingenious, if unorthodox, solution: through the use of triangular vault cells, visually unified by articulating ribs rather than more conventional quadripartite vaults, he was able to ensure a regular and harmonious covering for the space **(fig. 7)**.

The rest of the plan of the cathedral of Paris likewise resulted from simple geometrical formulas, even though the realization of these designs was far from simple. The logic of the project responded, first and foremost, to liturgical demands, which could not be interrupted for any reason: a functional, covered space of sufficient size was always required. Until the completion of the new chevet, the old cathedral served this purpose.

The Construction

Once the site for the new chevet was cleared, the next step was to lay foundations that were deep and wide enough to prevent the building from shifting. In fact,

1170

Building the Cathedral

faulty foundations were the leading cause of major structural problems in Gothic buildings. At Notre Dame, the foundations were laid on the sand using large blocks of stone to distribute the weight. The foundations were not built on stilts, as was long maintained. Large blocks were cut from the strongest possible stone—in this case, rock—probably from the open-air quarries in the Bièvre river valley. The foundations could then be filled with stone from the old cathedral **(fig. 8)**.

After the foundations, the walls and piers soon followed. The plan, until this point expressed through lines, geometric forms, and gaping trenches filled with blocks of stone, would then have to be defined: it was now necessary to articulate the form of the bases **(fig. 9)**, piers, and arcades. We often imagine the cathedral as a massive spatial composition, whose plan is taken to be the expression of the artistic genius of the mason. And yet the expression of this genius reveals itself as often in the details as in the overall scheme. How did the master mason explain to the workers what he envisioned for the smallest details?

No working drawings survive from before the mid-thirteenth century. Architectural drawings from later periods suggest that their primary function was not to guide the construction project on site but rather to be presented to the patron, although it is hard to generalize based on such a limited number of examples.

There is no evidence that drawings were made in the twelfth century for the cathedral of Paris. However, it is likely that the master mason gave a series of verbal instructions that may have been transcribed: first, the overall scheme, via sketches possibly executed on a plaster surface, and then on a more detailed level for the capitals, the molding profile of the bases or ribs, with the aid of a series of panels traced with a compass, rule, and square. As these were representations in two dimensions of complex three-dimensional forms, individual variations were to be expected in light of the individual stonemasons working at the site—in fact, they were inevitable. If we examine the building carefully, we can detect these variations from the overall scheme the master mason conceived. Not all of these changes

8. The excavations undertaken in the nave in 1983 revealed that the stones of an earlier structure were used in the foundations; under the Gothic structure, here are fragments of two mid-twelfth-century colonnettes from an embrasure.

9. Bases of the colonnettes of an ambulatory pier, south side.

resulted from individuals diverging from models provided: the forms used in the design of the cathedral were under constant revision. The critical eye of all of the individuals present at the site, including the stonemasons, the master mason, and perhaps even the bishop and chapter, meant that any drawings would evolve rapidly.

Who were the workers responsible for building the cathedral? In the absence of twelfth-century payment registers concerning the cathedral, we cannot be certain, but given the relative speed of construction, several hundred individuals were likely involved **(fig. 10)**. There were mortarers (who prepared the mortar), masons (who laid the stones), stone carvers, roofers, smiths, leadworkers, carpenters, and members of other specialized trades as well as handlers and carters, who were

the most numerous at the building site. The number of workers, most of them itinerant, fluctuated according to changes in the rhythm of construction, resulting from supply problems or financial obstacles, as well as seasonal hazards (laying mortar was, for instance, prohibited in the winter months). Based on what we can deduce from a remarkable document called *The Book of Trades*, compiled by Étienne Boileau, provost of Paris, around 1260, workers were probably organized in guilds. Each trade had a set of rules to follow—for example, masons had to undergo an apprenticeship of at least six years—and any breach could lead to a sanction.

The stone came in numerous varieties, corresponding to the various layers of limestone available **(fig. 11)**. The stone that came from the Parisian quarries was generally of excellent quality; the delicate

1170
Building the Cathedral

10. The depiction of the construction of the Temple in Jerusalem offered the painter an occasion to detail, in the foreground, the transport and the working of stone as well as the preparation of mortar. Master of the Munich Boccaccio, *Antiquités judaïques*, ca. 1470 (Paris, BnF, ms Fr. 247, fol. 163).

isotropic layer called *liais*, for instance, was highly sought after throughout the royal domain. The imperative to use the highest-quality stone in the construction of the cathedral resulted not only from the bishop and chapter's desire to construct the most beautiful edifice possible but also from ease of access. The stone used above the level of the foundations in the chevet probably came from one of the open-air quarries along the banks of the Seine, like those that existed in Charenton and Saint-Maurice. The master mason and stonemasons were well aware of the structural and

sculptural properties of the different types of stone. Stones were selected based on their size, resistance to friability, and their ability to be sculpted, as well as their color and texture, among other criteria. The capitals of the choir arcade, for example, were realized in *cliquart* stone, cut into blocks that weighed nearly three tons each, roughly hewn at the quarry to facilitate their transport to the site. The arches and ribs of the vaults, for their part, were made of liais or cliquart, depending on where along the incline they were placed (and the resulting constraints); the keystones of the

11. Former underground quarry beneath the Gravelle plateau, Île-de-France (Coll. SEHDACS). Similar quarries provided the stone for the cathedral.

vaults were made of *lambourde*. Since some of these elements required a long time to sculpt, they would be carved in advance and stored before being installed; for this reason, it is not always possible to determine the construction chronology based solely on the style of the sculpture.

We have just traced the underlying approach to the conception and construction of the chevet. Yet there remains one element crucial to the construction's success: the structure. How was the master mason certain that the new cathedral of Paris would stand up? In fact, he could not have been sure and had recourse only to his intuition. The moment of truth came during the construction of the vaults, which demanded more of the building than simply holding up the walls. It is to this subject that we will turn in the next chapter. ◆

The choir and the chevet of the cathedral are complete, except for the high vaults. The roof and wooden framework were constructed before the vaults, not only because they offered protection from the rain but also because the roof trusses provided a platform from which to place the centering and the stones of the vaults. The flying buttresses were built in anticipation of the vaults; their thrust against the outer wall was countered by the vault centering. In fact, in light of the unusual length of the flying buttresses (and their concomitant weight), the upper wall bowed inward at several points prior to the installation of the vaults. Work continues in the transept and in the first bays on the south side of the nave.

1177

1177

Constructing the Vaults

The Vaults

In a chronicle of 1177, the abbot of Mont-Saint-Michel, Robert de Torigni, recorded that the construction of the new cathedral of Paris was progressing rapidly and that the chevet was complete except for its covering, by which he meant not the roof but the vaults. The most common practice was to erect the roof as soon as the outer walls were in place: not only would the roof protect the building from the elements, but it could also serve as a platform from which to perform the most perilous operation: the construction of the vaults.

Putting up the walls was a relatively straightforward operation. The blocks of stone were cut in the desired dimensions at the quarry, and then small adjustments were made at the building site. Next, the blocks were laid in courses, ensuring that they were well aligned at critical junctures, such as the base of the windows. Masonry structures are extremely resistant to compressive forces. The stone, after all, simply continues to do what it has always done: that is, stay in a bed under intense pressure from the weight of the stone on top of it. However, all certainty evaporates as soon as lateral forces are introduced.

Inside, the vaults may give the impression that they are monolithic structures resting on the walls (and exerting vertical forces), but this is not the case. The principal role of the mortar of both the walls and the vaults consists of joining the masonry. The mortar joining the stones of a vault does not act as an adhesive. At most, it is somewhat resistant to friction, but it is powerless to resist against tension: that is, when two stones are pulled in opposite directions, even if a layer of mortar joins them, they will eventually separate. Under their own weight and due to the phenomenon of constant expansion and contraction caused by the freeze-thaw cycle, fissures will invariably appear in the vaults, forming a complex series of partial arcades, which exert a force on the upper part of the walls.

Left to their own devices, these strong thrusts would be shouldered by the upper walls of the building; in the cathedral of Maurice de Sully, they were transferred to a series of flying buttresses. Used in Gothic architecture for nearly three decades, this mechanism was meant to receive the thrusts from across the two aisles in a single span, so that they would definitely act on the massive *culées* (uprights) that received the flyers. Flying buttresses were the most effective way to support the building from the exterior while allowing the maximum amount of light to enter the building with

1. The chevet of Notre Dame seen from the Seine: flying buttresses transform the exterior of the building, creating a complex play of light and shadow.

a great economy of means; light, after all, was a material as essential as stone to the construction of the cathedral. It was not possible to erect traditional buttresses directly against the clerestory wall, or with a sufficient depth: they would have weighed down the vaults of the tribunes underneath and would have caused more damage than anything.

The introduction of flying buttresses had an important effect: it radically transformed the exterior elevation of Gothic buildings from an aesthetic point of view **(fig. 1)**. The stacked elevation of the early Christian basilica, a later medieval variant of which could still be found to the west of the new cathedral, was definitively abandoned, and the exterior became the site of complex play of light and shadow. The flying buttress was the most visible element of a structural system that also

1177

Constructing the Vaults

consisted of metallic ties. At Notre Dame, the cornice of the outer wall was, for example, fitted with a series of iron staples, which consolidated the upper wall in the face of thrusts **(fig. 2)**: not those of the vaults—which the flying buttresses absorbed—but those of the roof, subject to the intense force of the wind, whose speed increased according to its distance from the ground. Iron is the least visible element in Gothic buildings. It was most likely hidden for reasons more linked to its associations with the forge of hell than its relatively unsightly appearance. However, it was critically important to keeping in place this vast cage of Gothic light.

The purpose of these different elements, which the builders took for granted (particularly in the case of the flying buttresses), was not only to prevent the building from falling down but also to hold it in place. Various nonaxial thrusts could easily displace the lightweight masonry of Gothic buildings. Some sources show that being out of plumb was considered ungraceful, unworthy of the perfection that one would expect of a temple created in the image of the Heavenly Jerusalem. The early experiments in Gothic architecture, the first generation of cathedrals and abbey churches constructed in the new architectural style, in which curves and twists proliferated, taught the first master mason of Notre Dame an important lesson: if he wished to avoid these problems, he had to employ specific techniques to combat them.

In light of the fact that vaults were onerous and complex to build, and that they suffered all too often from faults in the lightweight masonry built to support them, we might begin to wonder why they were considered necessary. There are several possible responses to this question.

Vaults were durable: the cathedral, constructed in the image of heaven, was built to last. By enclosing the central vessel in stone, in the same material as the walls, the vaults gave the building a visual continuity, both longitudinally and laterally. From a practical point of view, the vaults were an effective way of battling the fires that regularly plagued medieval buildings and their immense wooden roofs. Notably, they prevented burning beams from falling into the main vessel. In addition, the resonant acoustical properties of such

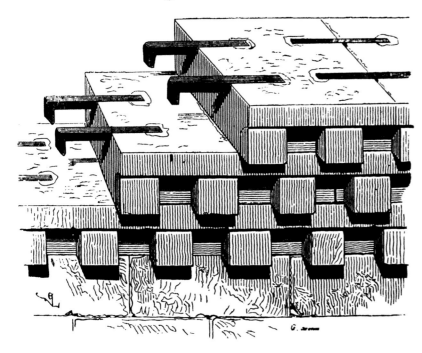

5

2. A series of iron ties links one stone of the original cornice of the choir to the next, as illustrated in the entry for "chaînage" from a volume of Eugène-Emmanuel Viollet-le-Duc's *Dictionnaire raisonné de l'architecture française du XIe au XVIe siècle*, published in 1856.

a space, conceived above all for the celebration of the Mass and Divine Office, were linked, for many, to the presence of these vaults.

Technical Aspects of Vault Construction

The art of vaulting can be summed up as the art of erecting the formwork that would hold the vaults in place during their construction **(fig. 3)**. It required large amounts of wood, which was felled in the woods belonging to the bishop and chapter and then transported to the site in the same manner as the stone. In his

text on the consecration of the abbey church of Saint Denis, Abbot Suger specifically mentions carpenters from Paris, who apparently enjoyed an excellent reputation at the time.

Unlike contemporary scaffolding, which is often put together on the ground and then raised to the desired height, medieval builders wanted to limit the expense of and time spent building such structures, making use of the walls to accomplish most of their task. To that end, they left holes in the walls in which they inserted wooden beams, used as levers. These openings, called putlog holes, were then reused when the building required repairs.

1177

Constructing the Vaults

3. The centering, suspended from the roof trusses, was designed to support the vault ribs. The ribs, in turn, served as formwork for the webbing of the vaults.

The formwork for the vault ribs was built first. The individual arch stones were placed on top and held in place by the keystone; it was then necessary to add the vault webbing, with the help of a series of suspended platforms and planks, in a complex three-dimensional composition. The haunches of the vaults were partially masonry to prevent them from caving in toward the top. After a certain length of time (difficult to determine retrospectively) came the moment of truth, the dismantling of the formwork: the wooden structure under the vaults was removed (and shifted to the next bay), and the structure was left to its own devices. The vaults fissured and exerted their thrust; the flying buttresses absorbed this force; the uprights and buttresses transferred it all to the ground. The structure survived the centuries without shifting. The results of the 3-D laser scan indicate that the upper walls have barely moved—a real feat, since the calculations of the master mason could only have been intuitive (fig. 4).

The Space of the Choir

The vaults crowned a series of spatial zones designed according to the equilateral triangle derived from the plan. On the lower level were double aisles; above, tribunes. A third level corresponded in height to the

4. Section of the choir generated from the laser scan. The upper wall has remained perfectly in plumb, as evidenced by the fact that it is parallel to the vertical edge of the image.

5. Choir tribunes, view from the southwest.

lean-to roof that covered the vaults of the tribunes. The oculi, a stylistic innovation, relieved the openings and aired out the dark space under the roofs, as if they had been cut out of the thin membrane of the wall. Finally, the high windows were placed above.

The function of the choir and aisles is clear: to support the celebration of the liturgy. But what about the tribunes **(fig. 5)**? If the presence of large spiral staircases seems to suggest that the liturgy likewise unfolded there, the hypothesis remains difficult to prove, due to

the lack of documentary evidence. On the other hand, the absence of an integrated system of railings leads us to believe that the tribunes were not used frequently; rather, they were spatial zones equal in dimension to the aisles they surmounted, extended upward to push the cathedral upward to the greatest possible extent, to the unexplored summits of Gothic architectural space.

This four-story elevation defined the design of the new cathedral of Paris. Next, we will see how it was subtly modified when work on the nave began. ◆

The choir, finished by 1182, is isolated from the active building site by a provisional wall. Construction continues from east to west in the transept and the nave.

1182

1182
Liturgical Choir and Sanctuary

On May 19, 1182, roughly twenty years after construction began, the clergy took control of the east end of the cathedral. The legate Henri, cardinal of Albano, presided over the ceremony and consecrated the high altar located at the end of the central vessel, directly below the keystone of the vault of the hemicycle.

The Liturgical Choir

At that point, the clergy occupied the four straight bays of the choir, immediately east of the crossing, just before the sanctuary situated in the apse of the central vessel **(figs. 1–3)**. Joining the bishop and the fifty-one canons of the cathedral chapter were several dozen chaplains who assisted them in the services, as well as clerics and choirboys. The total number of clergy present could surpass one hundred people. Representatives of religious establishments closely linked to Notre Dame

1. The illustration for Pentecost in this Parisian Book of Hours from around 1420 (Los Angeles, J. Paul Getty Museum, ms 57, fol. 187v, detail) takes place in the choir of Notre Dame, which is recognizable from the depiction of the tribunes and clerestory windows. This is the oldest representation of the interior of the cathedral.

2. In the Middle Ages, the canons sat in the straight bays of the choir, and the high altar was placed in the sanctuary at the end of the apse. The slenderness of the superstructure reinforces the solemnity of this zone.

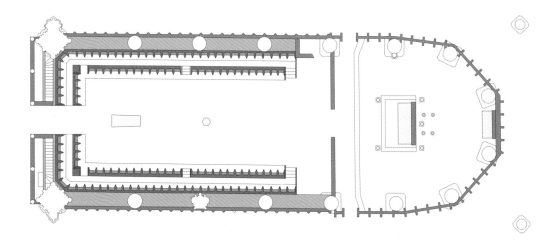

3. Plan of the liturgical choir.

1182

Liturgical Choir and Sanctuary

likewise had seats in the choir, as well as the six vicars of Saint-Maur, Saint-Martin-des-Champs, Saint-Victor, Saint-Marcel, Saint-Denis-de-la-Chartre, and the collegiate church of Saint-Germain-l'Auxerrois. On solemn feast days, the thirteen priests of the oldest parishes of the city, designated cardinals, assisted the bishop in the celebration of the Divine Office, on the model of the cardinals of the Roman Curia. The choir of Notre Dame therefore welcomed other communities that recognized its authority, but access was restricted to the clergy. The only laypeople authorized to enter the choir were kings and princes, who could enter to perform their devotions. At the center of the liturgical choir was situated, in line with the keystone of the first bay, the bronze tomb of Eudes de Sully, the first bishop to be interred in the Gothic cathedral in 1208. His effigy remained visible to later generations of canons and prelates until the eighteenth-century remodeling of the choir.

Mass was the main liturgical event of each day, which, with the eight canonical hours, formed nine offices, arranged into three periods of activity. One group took place at night (matins and lauds), another in the morning (prime, terce, Mass, and sext), and a third in the early evening (nones, vespers, and compline). If the Eucharist, one of the seven sacraments of the

4. The Porte Rouge takes its name from the color of the portal's door panels. Renovated around 1270, it offered the canons direct access to the choir from their living quarters nearby.

Church, gave the Mass its distinctive character, psalms, prayers, and chants comprised the canonical hours, varying according to the solemnity of the feast, and occupying a large part of the clergy's time. The morning hours began regularly at 8:00 a.m. and finished before noon; those of the afternoon ran from 3:30 to around 6:00 p.m. At Notre Dame, the clergy remained faithful to the tradition of celebrating matins at midnight. Canons and clerics had to get up in the middle of each night for this office, to which they were called by the ringing of a bell. They entered the cathedral at the third bay on the north side of the chevet, fitted around 1270 with an elegant portal, the Porte Rouge **(fig. 4)**. From there,

5. The sleeping soldiers at the tomb of Christ: a fragment of the Passion cycle (ca. 1230) that decorated the *jubé* positioned between the eastern crossing piers (Dépôt lapidaire de la cathédrale).

they reached the liturgical choir via a door inserted at the fifth bay of the choir on the same side. When the bishop attended the office, he came directly from the episcopal palace to the south of the cathedral via entrances directly opposite those of the chapter. Within the liturgical choir, the clergy sat in choir stalls arranged on two levels. Affixed to the back of the choir screen put up between the piers of the main vessel, at the west end of the choir the stalls wrapped around perpendicularly, positioned between the eastern crossing piers, from which they were blocked off by the stone *jubé*, or front of the choir screen **(fig. 3)**. Like the choir stalls that survive at Amiens and Poitiers Cathedrals, the stalls of Paris featured individual seats fitted with armrests, isolated from one another by partitions, and probably fitted with misericords from the beginning; when the seat was raised, this sculpted console under each seat provided a discreet perch that made the long periods spent standing (required by the celebration of multiple offices) less onerous. The wooden choir stalls were in place from the time the Gothic choir was inaugurated. The stalls were subject to repairs and updating over the centuries that followed, without fundamentally changing their original disposition **(fig. 6)**.

Staging the Ecclesiastical Hierarchy

At either end of the choir stalls sat the eight dignitaries of the church. The stall of the bishop and that of the chancellor were located closest to the sanctuary, at the east end. At the other end, the dean (head of the chapter) and the cantor (responsible for the liturgy) occupied the upper stalls, on either side of the entrance to the choir, piercing the partition enclosing the choir at the west end; the dean sat to the south, the cantor to the north. Seated next to them were the archdeacons, dignitaries of the chapter and delegates of the bishop, each responsible for part of the territory of the diocese: the archdeacons of Josas and Brie sat to the south, and the archdeacon of Paris sat to the north, between the cantor and the succentor.

6. In this representation by Jean Marot of the Te Deum celebrated in August 1660 for Louis XIV's wedding, the engraver omitted the *jubé* to make the image more legible, revealing the U-shaped disposition of the choir stalls on two levels (Musée Carnavalet).

1182

Liturgical Choir and Sanctuary

The forty-three other canons were, quite literally, "installed" in the remaining seats. The most distinguished—the priests and deacons—occupied the upper stalls, and the rest occupied the lower stalls. With seniority, the canons benefitted from a kind of physical advancement, which brought them closer to either the sanctuary or the west end of the choir where the dignitaries were seated. The space left empty between the lower stalls could be occupied by those reciting or chanting in the services, vicars, minor canons, and clerics of the choir (called *machicots*); all of this followed a precisely codified hierarchy that respected the strict symmetry of south and north, the respective sides where the Epistle and the Gospel were read. The choirboys and beneficed clerics who were not yet ordained were seated on benches placed on the ground.

The singers had two stands for choir books, situated at the center of each row of lower choir stalls, on both the north and the south. A large copper lectern for liturgical books is documented at the end of the fourteenth century. Books indispensable to the celebration of the offices were kept there. An inventory of 1409 details that to prevent theft, psalters, large graduals, and antiphoners were chained on both sides of the choir. On the most solemn feasts—Christmas, Epiphany, the Purification of the Virgin, Candlemas (commemorating the Presentation of Jesus in the Temple), Easter, Pentecost, Corpus Christi, Assumption, the Nativity of the Virgin, Saint-Denis, All Saints—the cantor directed the choir himself, assisted by three singers. On the other feasts, between one and four choir masters (*rectores chori*) chosen from among the minor canons of the neighboring churches of Saint-Denis-du-Pas and Saint-Jean-le-Rond carried out this duty.

The isolation of the choir sheltered by the choir screen gave the space specific acoustical properties, which had an effect on the liturgy, particularly on its sung portion **(figs. 7–8)**. Due to the difference in the acoustics inside and outside the choir—with a shorter reverberation time in the choir due to the reduced dimensions of the space and the presence of a number of absorbent materials (choir stalls, tapestries, etc.)—plainchant and polyphony were interpreted in a unique way. It was there that scholarly polyphony, composed at Notre Dame beginning at the end of the twelfth century by composers including Léonin and Pérotin, key figures in the Notre Dame school of polyphony, could shine

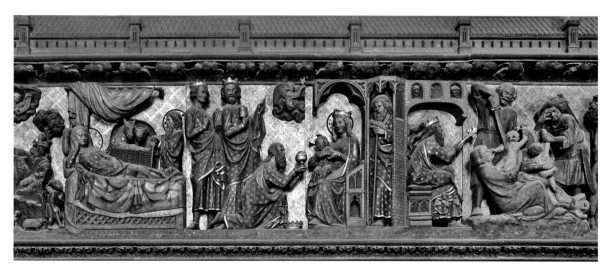

7 and 8. On its exterior, the masonry screen of the liturgical choir features an elaborate iconographic cycle dedicated to the Virgin Mary and the Life of Christ on the north side and post-Resurrection appearances of Christ on the south side (late thirteenth to early fourteenth century).

1182

Liturgical Choir and Sanctuary

the most brightly. On the most solemn feast days, the chants were more numerous. The increased light used on these occasions may have also made it easier to follow directions. Moreover, the absorptive properties of the elaborate ornaments endowed the acoustics with greater clarity.

The Medieval Sanctuary

Elevated by several steps since the beginning, the sanctuary occupied the east end of the central vessel. The high altar was located there; the most precious sacred objects were concentrated there. The place where the High Mass was celebrated, the high altar consisted of a table on which were placed the liturgical implements—chalice, paten, and cruets, as well as the books necessary for the celebration of the Mass. To these liturgical implements were added ornaments, stationary or portable, made of textiles or precious metals, such as antependia, altar frontals that hid what was behind them, or retables (literally *retro tabula*), a type

9 and 10. The vault of the apse contains a keystone featuring a cross and a sphere.

of furniture placed at the back of the altar table. The celebrant stood before the altar, turning his back to the clergy who witnessed the office from the liturgical choir. The celebrant found himself in line with the keystone of the hemicycle vault, decorated with the image of a cross, recalling Christ's sacrifice, which the priest recreated through the Eucharistic sacrament. A sphere decorated with a cross, occupying the obtuse angle of the vault ribs on the west side of the hemicycle vault recalled the universal authority of Christ, which the clergy enjoyed on earth **(figs. 9–10)**.

The altar itself was dedicated to the Virgin Mary, the patron saint of the cathedral. This symbiosis is illustrated perfectly in the *Book of Sermons*, on which each

11. Virgin and Child from the *Book of Sermons* of the Paris cathedral chapter, ca. 1250 (Archives nationales, LL 79, fol. 3). It was on this illumination that bishops and canons took the oath of office on the day of their installation.

new canon, as well as the bishop, vowed to defend the rights of the Church of Paris. The Virgin in Majesty is solemnly represented seated not on a throne but on an altar, recognizable as a stone with two candlesticks placed on top **(fig. 11)**. The Infant Christ she carries holds an orb in his hand. A century later, this emblematic image, painted around 1250, remained faithful to the symbolism of the Church, embodied by both the Virgin and the altar of the cathedral.

From the beginning, the principal altar of Notre Dame attracted the attention of the wealthiest donors, kings, bishops, and other prelates. Maurice de Sully adorned it with an altar frontal in gold. Dean Barbedor offered, around 1180, manuscripts bound in metalwork bindings for the reading of sacred texts. Louis VII donated a golden chalice weighing 2.5 marks (about 600 grams) for the daily High Mass. It may have been for the high altar that his son Philip II Augustus donated

1182

Liturgical Choir and Sanctuary

a retable, as well as other ornaments. Queen Ingeborg donated a sumptuous textile (pallium) of embroidered red samite to serve the altar.

Over the course of the Middle Ages, the high altar was subject to significant changes. We know through descriptions and account books its state in the second half of the fourteenth century; it remained more or less the same until 1699, when the vow of Louis XIII was made in 1638. The altar looked like a stone casket with a base articulated by arcades featuring pointed arches, in which were placed relics to reinforce its sacred character. Behind it, around 1340, a large retable in gilded silver by the goldsmith Jean de Montpellier was installed; on it were represented the Coronation of the Virgin (patron of both the cathedral and the altar), the Annunciation, Saint Stephen (another patron of the church), and Saint Marcel (the bishop of Paris, d. 436, whose relics were kept in a shrine nearby). Crowning these high-relief repoussé figures were pinnacles made of the same material. A metalwork altar frontal is likewise documented at the end of the fourteenth century.

In the fourteenth century, the consecrated host was suspended above the altar: a silver-gilt tabernacle was hung from a copper hook fitted into a colonnette made of the same metal, itself fixed just behind the altar table. It was lowered by a hand-cranked mechanism that caused a cable to wrap around a bobbin, a process not without difficulties, if we are to judge by the frequency of repairs to this mechanism. A large silver cross with a crucifix in gilded silver surmounted the high altar. It was isolated on either side by curtains hung on rods placed at the top of the copper colonnettes crowning angels carrying the Instruments of the Passion. This device, visible only to the clerics seated in the liturgical choir, helped maintain the solemnity of the sanctuary during the celebration of the offices.

At the back of the sanctuary, against the axial bay of the apse, was positioned the altar of the Trinity, also called the altar *des ardents* **(fig. 3)**. It took its name from a miracle that occurred in 1128 in the previous cathedral, the healing of numerous people suffering from ergotism, or *mal des ardents*, thanks to the intercession

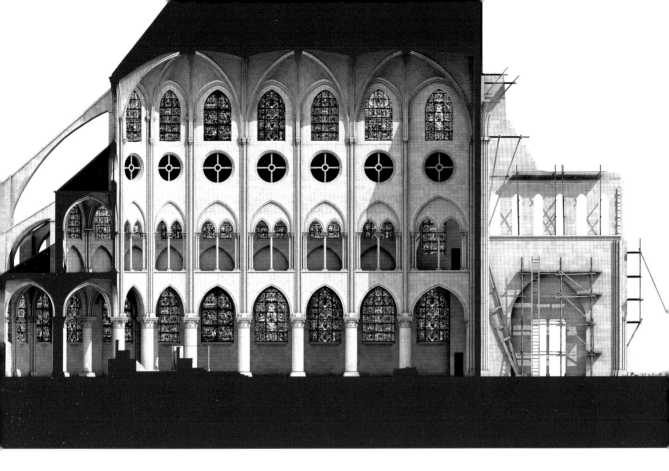

of Saint Genevieve, whose shrine was brought there from the eponymous abbey located on the Left Bank. A painted panel, an exceptional vestige of the medieval decoration of the cathedral choir, served in the fifteenth century as a retable for this altar: flanking God the Father, Christ, and the dove of the Holy Spirit (constituting the Trinity, to which the altar was dedicated), we find two groups of canons clad in white surplices with amices draped over their forearms and kneeling in prayer **(see page 11, fig. 6)**. This representation of

12. Longitudinal section of the choir, with a hypothetical reconstruction of the original elevation: the oculi of the third story are ornamented with large sculpted crosses alluding to the presence within the cathedral of a relic of the True Cross.

the college of canons, a pendant to the effigy of Bishop Eudes de Sully over his tomb at the entrance to the choir, marked the limit of a space reserved strictly for the clergy. ◆

The transept is now finished,
with façades whose upper parts
feature large rose windows,
reimagined here on the model
of the rose window of Vaux-de-
Cernay Abbey. Work continues
in the nave, and the bases of the
great west towers are begun.
The changes to the design visible
inside the nave are also reflected
on its exterior: the uprights of the
flying buttresses are taller, and
the flyers themselves are sturdier,
probably to offer greater stability.

1208

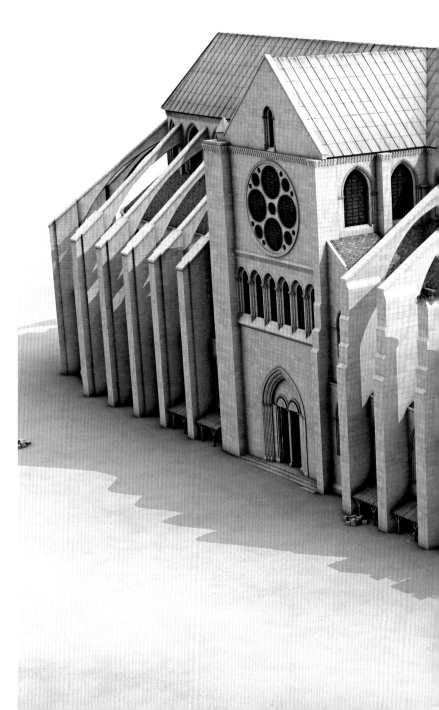

1208

Form and Meaning

Inspired by Sens and Senlis Cathedrals, the master mason of Notre Dame decided to construct vaults in the central vessel that would link two adjacent bays, rather than covering each individual bay, as in the aisles and tribunes **(fig. 1)**. In this decision, we might see a desire for the new building to follow in the footsteps of important precursors, and also to create a spatial hierarchy: the central vessel, where most of the liturgy unfolded, received a covering quite different from that of the tribunes and aisles; its importance was likewise evident in the keystones of the vaults, the capitals, the moldings, and even the plinths.

1. Sexpartite vaults of the choir seen from below; at left is the hemicycle vault.

1208
Form and Meaning

In the main vessel, the thin ribs, composed of two tori and a fillet, cover the sharp edges of the vaults and make legible what would otherwise be a series of indistinct curves. Perhaps the builder is inviting us to see in them lines of force, the symbolic journey of the thrust of the vault toward the wall—all the while knowing perfectly well that the ribs do not support the vaults. More likely, however, these delicate lines traversing the vaults and extending down the walls in the form of colonnettes—the responds—were designed to reinforce the conceptual space of the building, its architectonic essence, creating a formal interplay of lines visible to all.

Each vault is divided into six parts, from which comes the term "sexpartite vault." The vaults do not spring from every capital, but rather from every other capital, producing a syncopated rhythm in the vaulting that primes us to expect a similar syncopation in the rhythm of the responds. This is the case above the high capitals: every other capital receives five elements (two ribs, two formerets, and one transverse arch), whereas the rest only receive one (a transverse rib).

However, below this level, the master mason of Notre Dame decided to break with these conventions: the responds are uniform, the alternating system in

2. Elevation of the north wall of the choir, seen from the tribunes of the nave.

evidence in the vaults having been ignored here—an unusual choice that seems to have resulted from the desire to highlight the mural surfaces.

The canonical features of the Corinthian order that define the relationship between the capital, the shaft, and the base of the columns are elongated in the responds; the graceful aspect that results accentuates both the impression of height and the flatness of the wall **(fig. 2)**. This attenuation is echoed in the undulating bundles of colonnettes that serve to disguise the massiveness of the structure at the level of the tribune and in the *en-délit* shaft that divides each bay of the tribune. Place- ment *en délit* means that the natural grain of the stone is placed vertically (perpendicularly). The builders were beginning to see that long shafts of isotropic stone—fine- grained stone that could be loaded from any direction— offered a wide range of interesting possibilities. Using stones placed *en délit* would soon become widespread in the world of Gothic construction; the presence of such shafts at the level of the tribunes at Notre Dame indi- cates the confidence and nascent interest in a new and relatively unexplored method. Elsewhere in the choir, the columns are coursed into the wall. If we follow the responds down the wall, we encounter a surprise: the planar surface and its gracious linearity are abruptly interrupted above the abaci of the arcade capitals, which rest on massive cylindrical piers. Today, we are desensi- tized to this visual shock, since we are now accustomed to it (we perceive it more clearly in the nave **[fig. 3]**, since the choir piers are now hidden behind the choir screen). But to contemporaries, the effect would have been striking. It seems to have resulted from the desire to bring together old and new. The colonnade referenced

3. The central vessel of the nave, facing east.

1208
Form and Meaning

the ancient world. It recalls basilicas of the Constantinian era (fourth century), which had an impact on the form of all Christian buildings on this site up to its most recent version, the old cathedral then being dismantled to make space for the new nave. This novel combination of columns and vaults is in a mode that first arose at the abbey church of Saint-Denis under specific circumstances: the master mason of Abbot Suger arrived at this solution to link the nave of the Carolingian building with the newly constructed chevet. Perhaps we should also consider a symbolic meaning: the new element rises up from the columns, yet without detaching from them.

The Nave

Construction on the nave began while the choir was still being built. If the basic design remained the same, important changes were also introduced. Some resulted from innovations and technological progress, likely at the initiative of a new master mason. For example, in the choir, the vaults are relatively bulbous—that is, they are higher than the outer walls, to the point that the crowning of the vaults surpasses the height of the original wall **(fig. 4)**. This mode of vault construction, practiced in the Île-de-France since the 1140s, was probably preferred for its presumed structural advantages. In the nave, the longitudinal cells of the vaults are flatter, evident in a longitudinal section of the building **(fig. 5)**. The height under the vaults likewise increases beginning with the westernmost bay of the choir.

Another notable difference between the choir and the nave is the increase in the size and regularity of the blocks of stone used to build the walls. Even if the blocks were now too large to be manipulated by hand (as had previously been the case in the choir), the new mode of construction presented significant advantages in terms

4. The space under the roof covering the high vaults of the choir facing east, before the fire of 2019. The twelfth-century wall reached the level of the base of the consoles that receive the braces of the crossbeams.

1208
Form and Meaning

of the speed of construction. Moreover, there were fewer joints, increasing the stability of the walls.

The changes made to the plan of the nave should also be seen in the light of the formation of a spatial hierarchy. Just as the choir followed an internal organization, a hierarchical relationship may also be observed between the choir, the liturgical center accessible only to the bishop, canons, and those responsible for the celebration of the liturgy, and the nave, the part of the building accessible to all.

The distinction is immediately visible at the level of the transept crossing piers **(fig. 6)**: to the east are clusters of colonnettes, similar to the ones marking the bay divisions at the east end; each one corresponds to a rib or transverse arch after a brief interruption at the level of the high capitals. On the west side of the crossing, what appear to be pilasters are actually dosserets without shafts, now exposed to view. Here we find a stripped-down version of the choir. The treatment of the piers at the level of the tribune is similar **(fig. 7)**. In the choir, as we have seen, a bundle of shafts surrounds the pier; in the nave, they are absent, revealing the underlying structure. The result is that the bays of the tribunes are wider and divided into three openings instead of two.

The diameter of the columns marking these divisions were reduced by roughly 25 percent (from 26 centimeters in the choir to 20 centimeters in the nave), proof that the static properties of stone placed *en délit* were now better understood. In the choir, the use of

5. Longitudinal section, generated from the laser scan, of the vaults and the upper walls of the entire structure on the south side. The choir is at left (rounded vaults), and the nave is at right.

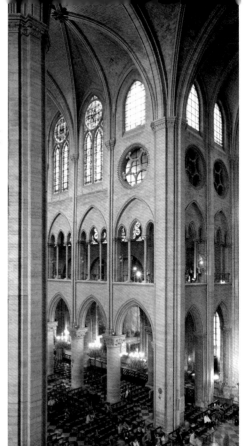

6. North elevation of the nave, as seen from the choir tribunes.

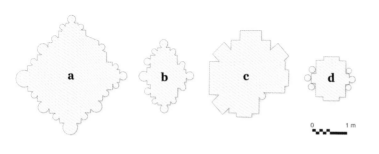

a   b   c   d

0   1 m

7. Comparative sections of the supports at the level of the tribunes: (a) southeast crossing pier; (b) choir pier one bay east of the crossing; (c) southwest crossing pier; (d) nave pier one bay west of the crossing.

1208
Form and Meaning

en-délit shafts was limited to the colonnettes of the tribune; in the nave, all of the colonnettes were realized with *en-délit* shafts, with the exception of those of the westernmost bay. The colonnettes covering the surfaces of the nave walls were even thinner than those of the choir, and their intrinsic hierarchy, established by the structure of the vault surmounting them, was eliminated: their diameters are similar. The differentiation of these elements, which creates a new play of light, also highlighted the apparent planarity of the wall by indicating that it continues behind, an effect that would reinforce the uninterrupted trajectory of the colonnettes, which cross the base of the tribunes as well as the abaci of the capitals articulating the tribune arcade. (It is important to note that the band at the base of the clerestory windows was not installed until the 1220s.) The colonnettes of the nave, now independent from the wall, fully took on their role as key elements in the articulation of the nave.

The archivolts of the relieving arches of the tribunes and those of the main arcade (which are doubled) were placed diagonally, against a chamfered border—identical to that of the oculi pierced on the south side; perhaps an attempt, if relatively timid, to allow more light to enter the building. Overall, the moldings are subordinated to the prismatic and simplified system to which they are attached. In the aisles, the abaci of the responds are flat against the wall; the colonnette in the middle is engaged, the dosseret barely discernible since its corners are heavily chamfered—another subtle reminder of the prismatic architectural vocabulary that predominates in this part of the building.

The alternation in the vaults of the central vessel find an unusual expression in the aisles, with an audacious use of *en-délit* colonnettes, which envelop every other pier **(fig. 8)**. It is here, it would seem, that we find the many "missing" responds of the strong piers of each sexpartite vault. A subtler expression of this

8. Double aisle on the north side of the nave, facing west.

alternating system (almost imperceptible to the naked eye) is in evidence in the piers of the third arch from the crossing, on the north and south, known as "weak" piers (they receive only the transverse rib of the sexpartite vault surmounting them): their diameter was reduced by 8 centimeters (from 1.33 meters to 1.25 meters). This modification was abandoned in the remaining weak piers as construction continued westward.

We have just described the macrocosmic distinctions between the choir and nave made in the name of creating a spatial hierarchy. If we were to examine in detail, on the microcosmic level, the capitals, the abaci, and the different moldings decorating the bases, we would discover that the same distinctions likewise apply at that scale. Every element served to delimit different zones of the cathedral's spatial envelope. ◆

The body of the cathedral is complete except for the upper part of the towers, with the west façade built up only to the level of the rose window.

1220

1220

Portals and the Gallery of Kings

The west front of Notre Dame was by far the most monumental structure in medieval Paris. With a width of 40 meters and towers 69 meters in height, it was one of the most ambitious frontispieces at the time of its construction in the first half of the thirteenth century. Out of scale with respect to the surrounding houses, it was one of the major landmarks of Paris, visible from well beyond the city limits. As such, it also expressed the protective role of the cathedral that had to make its mark on the broader landscape—namely, the region constituting the diocese. Once in the city, visitors would only see Notre Dame intermittently, from the labyrinth of narrow streets or from the riverbanks. The façade was not visible except from the end of the rue

1. The three portals surmounted by the monumental gallery of kings form a solemn entrance to the cathedral. The jamb figures are modern, but the rest (the archivolts, lintels, and tympana) is largely medieval.

Neuve-Notre-Dame, which Bishop Maurice de Sully had pierced along the building's axis, to the west, reaching the Petit-Pont. The street, one of the most frequented in Paris, was no less narrow: it was only upon reaching the plaza of no more than 30 meters in depth that it was possible to have an uninterrupted view of a façade so close that it must have seemed to hang over the viewer. At the rear of a shallow plaza encumbered with stalls where candles, books, and food were sold, and where a shady population intermingled with the faithful who came to visit the great church, the three portals offered a visual distillation of essential religious dogma, particularly explicit in its position on the Last Judgment, in the center portal, and on the protective presence of the Virgin Mary, accompanied by certain saints venerated at the cathedral **(fig. 1)**.

1220

Portals and the Gallery of Kings

The three portals, separated by buttresses, formed a veritable triumphal entrance to the church, an allegory for heaven. In the trumeau of the center portal **(figs. 2–3)**, Christ blesses and welcomes the faithful. It is a literal depiction of a parable from the Gospels (John 10:9: "I am the door. By me, if any man enter in, he shall be saved"), a fundamental text that promised heavenly rewards. The representation of the Wise and Foolish Virgins on the jambs also came from the Gospels (Matthew 25:1–13), positive and negative examples that echo the vices and virtues of the embrasures: the former are depicted in medallions featuring violent scenes illustrating the excesses to which they lead; the latter are symbolized by majestic enthroned female figures. The contrast between the disordered attitude of the vices and the serenity of the allegories of the virtues have a parallel above, in the twelve figures of the apostles situated in the jambs, holding the instruments of their martyrdoms and trampling their tormentors underfoot.

The upper half of the portal dramatizes the end of time. Above the bodily resurrection on the lintel

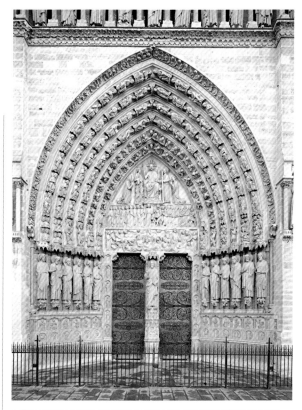

2. The center portal devoted to the Last Judgment features two representations of Christ: as judge at the end of time in the tympanum, and welcoming the faithful in the trumeau, at the entrance of a church symbolizing heaven.

3. Center portal: the oblique angle of the embrasures and archivolts emphasizes the vertical line linking the trumeau, lintels, and tympanum.

(modern), the archangel Michael weighs the souls: based on the weight of their sins, he separates the elect from the damned, under the authority of Christ of the Last Judgment, enthroned at the top of the tympanum. Flanking him are two angels holding the Instruments of the Passion, and the Virgin, with Saint John, intercedes on behalf of humankind. The damned are led to hell— which occupies the first voussoirs on the right—in a heap of tortured bodies, where we recognize among them a king and a bishop suffering the most awful punishments, crushed under the weight of a naked creature. The elect wait patiently to enter Paradise, where the patriarch Abraham has already received several souls. The heavenly host of angels, patriarchs, virgins, and kings radiates out from the central figure of Christ.

The overall composition, admirably organized, was conceived of by masters of theology of the Notre Dame school, who insisted on the necessity not of simply practicing the virtues but of letting oneself be guided entirely by them. This explains the imagery related to mortality, which served as the foundation for the instruction of the faithful as attested by contemporary preaching, which was very successful.

The portals were originally painted. Therefore, the figures would have been more legible, stood out more clearly from the background, and been more distinguishable from neighboring sculptures; some were trimmed with gold. Certain details would have been emphasized, particularly in the scenes depicting hell, through the use of bright colors, like the

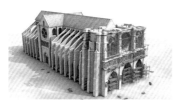

1220

Portals and the Gallery of Kings

red-orange that would have stood out from the more muted ochre tones.

The two lateral portals are largely devoted to the Virgin Mary, patron of the cathedral. On the north portal **(fig. 4)**, she is featured in the trumeau (redone in the nineteenth century), towering over the figure of Eve, whose sin she redeemed. In the embrasures, she is joined by Saint John the Baptist, Saint Stephen, and other figures venerated in the diocese, including Saint Genevieve and Saint Denis. Representing the great abbeys dedicated to these saints and who, in theory, were supposed to serve the cathedral dedicated to Mary, these figures form a procession toward the image of the mother of God. Above the trumeau figure, a canopy frames a depiction of the Ark of the Covenant; in the Temple of Jerusalem, this chest contained the Tablets of the Law God handed down to Moses. Here, kings and

4. The Coronation of the Virgin portal, at the base of the north tower, has a regular composition, as evidenced by the radial arrangement of the voussoirs.

high priests guard it. The Virgin, having carried Christ, was thus likened to the Ark in the typological symbolism common in the Middle Ages, which saw prefigured in the stories of the Old Testament the episodes of the New Testament. In the tympanum, amidst angels and heavenly bodies, the patron of the cathedral lies on her deathbed, surrounded by mourning apostles and in the presence of Christ. Two angels lift up the edges of the shroud to transport the Virgin to heaven. Here, in a single scene, is summarized the Dormition and Assumption of Mary, one of the most important feasts celebrated at Notre Dame since the Middle Ages. At the top of the tympanum, the Coronation of the Virgin marks her triumph in the next world.

The south portal, or the Saint Anne portal **(fig. 5)**, features some scenes relative to the mother of Mary on the lower lintel, but for the most part it relates again to the Virgin herself, with most of the sculptures reused from an old portal dating to the mid-twelfth century. The upper lintel presents scenes from the infancy of the Virgin and of Christ, the tympanum a triumphal vision of the Virgin, enthroned between angels and honored by a bishop and a king. Depictions of angels, prophets, and patriarchs populate the archivolts. The jamb figures, likewise redone in the nineteenth century by Viollet-le-Duc and his team, respects the original iconography in depicting Old Testament figures who predicted the

5. The Saint Anne portal, at the base of the south tower, integrates numerous elements from an older portal created in the mid-twelfth century for the previous cathedral.

coming of Christ, accompanied by Saints Peter and Paul (an explicit reference to papal power, of which they are the two patrons). The trumeau figure represents the founding figure Saint Marcel, bishop of Paris in the fifth century (the original sculpture is in the collection of the Musée de Cluny), piercing with the end of his crozier a dragon that had been terrorizing the outskirts of Paris by raiding tombs. That we find this figure, one of the most venerated at the Church of Paris, here is explained by the presence of his relics inside the cathedral, displayed from the end of the thirteenth century in a sumptuous

1220
Portals and the Gallery of Kings

6. Master of Saint-Gilles, *Saint Rémi Preaching*, ca. 1500 (Washington, D.C., National Gallery of Art, Samuel H. Kress Collection). At the end of the fifteenth century, the sculptures of the portals were more legible: polychromy made the figures stand out from dark backgrounds.

metalwork shrine placed above the cathedral's high altar. It also symbolized the protective role the bishops played from the beginning of the Church within the city and throughout the diocese.

The sculptural program, once brightly painted **(fig. 6)**, is punctuated by four buttresses with niches containing other patron saints of the Church of Paris: on the far left, Saint Stephen, another patron of the cathedral; on the far right, Saint Denis, its first bishop. Flanking the center portal are female personifications of Ecclesia and Synagoga: the former, crowned, proclaims victory over the latter, whose eyes are blindfolded, defeated. Here, too, Viollet-le-Duc respected, in its broad strokes, the original iconography planned by the medieval clergy, stigmatizing through anti-Jewish imagery the only non-Christian religion that could be practiced in the Middle Ages—not without risk to its followers, as evidenced by the exclusionary measures that proliferated from the end of the twelfth century. In 1183, Philip II Augustus confiscated a synagogue located near the cathedral and gave it to the bishop of Paris so that he could replace it with a church. This was the church of Saint Mary Magdalene (destroyed in the nineteenth

century, located on the site of the current Hôtel-Dieu), which quickly became the seat of the archpriesthood, which had authority over the priests of the Île de la Cité and the Right Bank. The façade of Notre Dame was the first place where monumental representations of Ecclesia and Synagoga appeared, repeated soon after at Reims, Strasbourg, and Bamberg.

7. With its twenty-eight statues, the gallery of kings is a pioneering sculptural ensemble glorifying royal power.

Crowning the three portals is an imposing gallery of kings **(fig. 7)**, a series of twenty-eight colossal statues, each more than three meters tall, redone by Viollet-le-Duc; many vestiges were found in 1977 and entered the collection of the Musée de Cluny **(fig. 8)**. It is the earliest surviving example of a monumental gallery of kings, soon taken up at Chartres, Amiens, and Reims Cathedrals. Between representation of the biblical kings of Israel and exaltation of the kings of France, it seems that we must favor the second option, which held sway in the Middle Ages: an anonymous chronicler of the mid-thirteenth century mocked the "country bumpkins" so absorbed in identifying Pepin the Short or Charlemagne that they were oblivious to the fact that they were being pickpocketed. To this literary account may be added an official document, the list of the kings of France since Clovis, affixed to the doors of the cathedral since at least this period. It was there that each new sovereign came, on the way back from the coronation in Reims, as he entered Paris to give his solemn vow before the bishop and chapter to respect and protect the privileges and liberties of the Church

8. Seven of the twenty-one heads discovered in 1977 from the gallery of kings (Musée de Cluny).

of Paris. Royal iconography also featured prominently on the lateral portals of the façade. In the tympanum repurposed from an earlier building, the depiction of a kneeling king seems to illustrate the investment of local political forces in the service of the Church, and the representation most likely postdates King Louis VI (1108–37), who did a great deal for the Paris cathedral clergy. On the opposite portal, underneath the depiction of the Coronation of the Virgin, the figures placed on the outer edges of the embrasures were, on the right, a pope,

◆ Sculpture of the West Portals ◆

North Portal, known as the Coronation of the Virgin portal

Center portal, known as the Last Judgment portal

1. Virgin and Child
2. Labors of the Months and Signs of the Zodiac
3. Jamb figures:
   a. Constantine, angel, Saint Denis, angel
   b. John the Baptist, Saint Stephen, Saint Genevieve, Pope Sylvester I

4. Prophets and kings flanking the Ark of the Covenant
5. Dormition and Assumption of the Virgin
6. Coronation of the Virgin
7. Angels, prophets, patriarchs, and Old Testament kings

1. Beau Dieu
2. Wise and Foolish Virgins
3. Vices and Virtues
4. Apostles
5. Resurrection of the Dead
6. Weighing of the souls and the separation of the elect from the damned (the edges of the lintel date to the thirteenth century, and the center was redone in the nineteenth century)

7. Hell and scenes from the Apocalypse
8. Heaven
9. Christ the Judge flanked by two angels bearing the Instruments of the Passion, the Virgin, and Saint John
10. Angels, prophets, patriarchs, martyrs, and virgins

 Medieval sculptures   Nineteenth-century restorations

South portal, known as the Saint Anne portal

1. Saint Marcel
2. Jamb figures
   a. Old Testament kings and queen, Saint Peter
   b. Saint Paul, David, Old Testament queen and king
3. Lintel and base of the archivolts
   a. Scenes from the Life of the Virgin: marriage of the Virgin, Annunciation, Joseph's doubt
   b. Scenes from the Life of Saint Anne and Joachim: rejection of offerings, separation, meeting at the Golden Gate
4. Scenes from the Life of the Virgin: the Virgin at the Temple, Isaiah, Annunciation, Visitation, Nativity, Annunciation to the Shepherds, the Magi before Herod
5. Virgin in Majesty between two angels, a king, a bishop, and a scribe
6. Angels, patriarchs, kings and elders of the Apocalypse
7. Lamb of God, Christ of the Apocalypse

9. Hypothetical reconstruction of the initial project for the west façade before the decision to add the gallery of kings.

and, opposite him, an emperor, likely Pope Sylvester I and Constantine, the first Christian Roman Emperor. In the eyes of medieval spectators, these figures illustrated the virtue of a political system in which royal power and ecclesiastical power were inextricably linked.

The gallery of kings, whose twenty-eight figures were, intentionally or not, double the number of jamb figures, suggests a desire around 1220 to underscore further the cathedral's royal dimension. This feature was not planned from the outset **(fig. 9)**, as its installation rendered necessary the thinning out of the masonry framing the portals, evidenced by the gable over the north portal and the projecting archivolts of the other two portals. What circumstances led to this major transformation of the façade? Added toward the end of the reign of Philip II Augustus, we might think of the prestige earned after his momentous victory in the Battle of Bouvines in 1214 over revolting barons and princes and English and Imperial enemies, which decidedly assured the authority of the Capetian

1220

Portals and the Gallery of Kings

sovereigns throughout Christendom. Parisians, who had financially and militarily supported their king in this operation, rejoiced for a week following the victory, after having welcomed the triumphant king, who exhibited his vanquished enemies—chief among them the count of Flanders, Ferrand of Portugal, who went on to spend several years imprisoned in the Louvre. Perhaps it was at this time that a statue of the king—still referenced by seventeenth-century historians before its removal when the choir was redone—was placed in the sanctuary.

At the end of the thirteenth century, the representation of the baptism of Clovis in the center of the gallery of kings at Reims Cathedral illustrated the continuity between a founding episode of the kingdom and the anointing ceremony (featuring the miraculous chrism of the Holy Ampulla). Around 1260, Louis IX introduced a kind of visible dynastic lineage at Saint-Denis, with the rearrangement of the royal tombs dating all the way back to the Merovingian dynasty. But from 1220, Notre Dame offered a gallery of kings wearing crowns and holding scepters—the attributes of the exercise of power. With the addition of polychromy, this sculptural ensemble formed a powerful image of the sovereigns who reigned nearby and reinforced a sense of dynastic continuity.

A large radial rose window occupies the center of the façade **(fig. 10)**. In the nineteenth century, it retained traces of paint: gold stars on a blue ground. In front of the rose window is a statue of the Virgin flanked by two angels, positioned high atop elevated bases. Documented since the sixteenth century, the original sculptures, redone later, likely dated to the thirteenth century. If the scale and appearance of the current figures are in line with the original statues, it is striking to notice that the figure of the Virgin is placed far in front of the rose window: when viewed from the medieval plaza below, the window itself would have formed a kind of nimbus for the central figure of the Virgin Mary. The edge of the medieval square is marked by a line in the modern pavement, roughly 35 meters west of the portals.

By seamlessly weaving the sculptural program into the architectural fabric, the façade of Notre Dame served an iconic function: it demonstrated on a grand scale that it was a monument both dedicated to the Virgin—mother of Christ and symbol of the Church—and protected by the kings subject to it. ◆

10. The façade, as seen from the back of the plaza, late seventeenth century (drawing by Antier, 1699, Paris, BnF).

Only a few years after its completion, the superstructure of the cathedral is partially dismantled in order to transform radically the clerestory windows. This operation gets under way while the towers of the cathedral are still under construction. At left, the retrofit of the choir has already been realized; the lean-to roofs of the tribunes and the oculi that once occupied this level of the elevation on the interior have been replaced by large windows featuring a double lancet surmounted by an oculus. New gabled roofs now cover the tribunes. The height of the wall of the central vessel was increased and a new roof built. The dismantling of the old roof continues at the west; the nave flyers are reworked, with channels being carved out from the extrados to drain rainwater from the main roof through the gutter at its base.

1225

1225

Changing Tastes

A Radical Transformation

In 1220, the bulk of the construction campaign launched by Bishop Maurice de Sully and overseen by his successors (Eudes de Sully, Pierre de Nemours, and Guillaume de Seignelay) and the cathedral chapter was finished. The western frontispiece had reached the base of the towers, and it had just been linked to the nave, a detail clearly indicated by the style of the piers: they reflect the mode of the *pilier cantonné*, popularized by Chartres

1. Main arcade of the first bays of the nave on the south side. The arch to the far right was put in place to link the nave to the structure of the tower, which explains its unusual form.

Cathedral and, even more recently, Reims Cathedral **(fig. 1)**. The use of *en-délit* shafts was abandoned in this bay, less for stylistic reasons than for structural ones: it was imperative to create a solid connection between, on the one hand, the longitudinal thrust of the vaults and the arcades of the last bay of the nave—maintained up to that point by a series of wooden platforms—and, on the other hand, the massive pile of the west front.

In the third decade of the thirteenth century, a precipitating event led to the radical renovation of the superstructure of the entire building. According to the architect Eugène-Emmanuel Viollet-le-Duc, who knew the edifice from top to bottom from having supervised the restoration campaign that unfolded over twenty years in the mid-nineteenth century, this event was a fire in the space between the vaults and the roof. Even before

1225

Changing Tastes

the 2019 fire, no trace of this fire remained. Perhaps this fire was linked to the serious damage that the decoration of the choir had suffered in 1218. This part of the building went up in flames after an English robber had knocked over some candles, having entered the space under the roof, from which he tried, through the use of ropes, to steal the silver chandeliers installed the day before the Feast of the Assumption.

This fire, assuming it was the same one, may have served as a pretext for the bishop and chapter to transform the building: the primary motivation behind the complete renovation of the superstructure, roofs, and flying buttresses was most likely to respond to a new mode of architectural production. Having been around for a mere sixty years, Notre Dame had already been eclipsed. Its height had long been surpassed, and the latest innovations in three-story elevations (tall arcade,

triforium, clerestory), housing remarkable cages of glass—in Soissons and Chartres Cathedrals, for example—made Notre Dame look somewhat outdated. The bishop and chapter, motivated by this climate of intense rivalry, decided to have large swaths of the as-yet-incomplete building dismantled. (Their counterparts at Laon Cathedral had just finished having that building's choir and sanctuary reconstructed, after having had the entire chevet demolished, even though it was only thirty years old.) This was a monumental overhaul, which mirrored the rising status of the cathedral and the capital city itself. Under the reign of Philip II Augustus, Paris became increasingly influential and was, more than ever, the administrative and artistic center of the expanding Capetian kingdom.

The Changes

The two principal changes made to the building were the doubling of the height of the clerestory windows **(fig. 2)** and the reconstruction of the main roofs, which led

2. The three-story elevation of the north side of the choir consists of a main arcade, tribune, and clerestory.

to an additional series of transformations at the level of the tribune roofs, a drainage system, and supporting mechanisms. The large bays of the new clerestory, composed of two lancets and a rose without petals, were designed based on those of the master mason Jean d'Orbais at Reims Cathedral, bringing Notre Dame up to date in terms of both style and construction technology. A new, uniform roof, higher in pitch and surmounted by a spire, gave the cathedral a verticality that was impossible to achieve otherwise. Of course, these changes also came with practical advantages. Larger windows with greater areas of glass allowed more light to enter the building; the new roof, placed on an outer wall raised to the same height in the choir and nave, along with a parapet, gutters, and a wall passage, addressed several other problems specific to tall buildings **(fig. 3)**. The roofs above the choir and nave, whose heights and slopes

1225

Changing Tastes

varied and whose connection to the crossing was improvised, were probably considered temporary. They were probably constructed in a summary manner, which may have compromised their stability (a hypothesis supported by the fact that the upper courses of the twelfth-century outer wall, as we saw, were fixed with iron ties). The relatively low level of the round-topped wall of the choir and the curvature of the vaults rendered impossible the construction of a roof with joists at the base of the triangle, the system offering the greatest stability.

The enlargement of the clerestory implied the suppression of the third story of the original elevation: the oculi were removed, and the base of the clerestory windows was lowered by 4.5 meters. New tracery with thin, *en-délit* elements and new stained glass were inserted. The level of the oculi, as we may recall, resulted

from the placement of the lean-to roof covering the tribune vaults; since this part was now replaced with glass, obviously the roof could no longer rest on the wall. It had to be transformed into a gabled roof, which had two major drawbacks: first of all, in order to create a uniform level for the new roof, the exterior wall of the tribunes had to be lowered by about 1.5 meters, which meant that the upper part of the tribune bays was truncated. Secondly, a roof with two slopes required the insertion of a gutter at the base of the new bays, practically inside the building—requiring constant monitoring for ice and other blockages.

Previously, the water drainage system placed at the level of the tribunes allowed water to drain not only from the roofs of the tribunes but also from the main roof, which drained directly down—that is, fully two-thirds

3. Comparative transverse sections of a bay of the choir (a) before modification and (b) after modification.

1225

Changing Tastes

of the rainwater that hit the building (excluding the towers). In the event of an average rainfall of 10 millimeters, for example, the drainage system of the tribunes had to be able to evacuate around 23,100 liters of water. It was, in part, an effort to minimize the quantity of water that would fall on the new roof of the tribunes, with its problematic gutter, that the flying buttresses of the choir were entirely rebuilt with drainage channels intended to funnel water from the main roof directly to the ground. In the nave, the buttresses were not reworked, with the exception of the flyers themselves, to which drainage channels and gargoyles were added.

Three flying buttresses were left completely untouched (two of which remained basically intact until 1846, when they were dismantled during the major restoration campaign). They were located at the southwest corner of the choir. The easternmost flying buttresses were spared because they were directly up against the two-story gallery that led to the episcopal palace (see the view in 1265, on pages 98–99); modifying the water drainage system at this point was probably deemed too complicated. The third flying buttress in question was hidden in the corner, and its drainage system was likewise difficult to rework.

Instability of the West Front

During this time, work on the façade continued largely without incident. And yet, behind its apparent regularity (whose subtleties we miss, since we are accustomed to its appearance), a veritable fight for its construction took place. An analysis of the laser scan of the west front reveals a wide array of formal anomalies that resulted from bad foundations, particularly on the north side **(fig. 4)**. The string course on which the gallery of kings rests, for example, is 30 centimeters higher at the south than it is at the north. In addition, if we consider whether the façade is in plumb, we find that the whole structure, up to the bases of the towers, has pivoted 30 centimeters outward, in the direction of the plaza

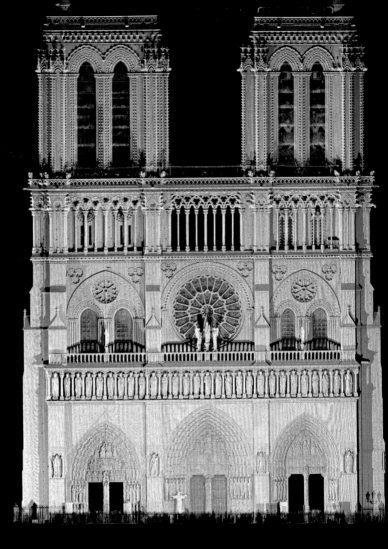

4. Elevation of the west façade generated from the laser scan. The leftward tilt of the lower parts of the façade resulted from unstable foundations.

1225
Changing Tastes

5. West façade, as seen from the north: the westward tilt of the structure is visible to the naked eye.

(fig. 5). It would seem that this displacement occurred toward the end of construction, when the ground was already heavily loaded with the mass of the edifice: there is no indication that an intervention was attempted to correct this imbalance. (The colonnettes of the gallery of kings and the large gallery under the towers were finally put back in plumb during the major restoration of the nineteenth century.) The additional thrust of the vaults of the westernmost bay of the nave, adjoined to the ensemble via this linking bay, certainly did not help, and this zone remains one of the most irregular parts of the entire building **(fig. 6)**.

It seems that work was interrupted for some time—perhaps resources were redirected to the reworking of the clerestory and the roof—while the master mason, chapter, and bishop anxiously waited to see what would

6. Elevation generated from the laser scan of the first two bays of the nave on the north side. The outward tilt of the west end is noticeable in the left pier.

happen, powerless to resolve a problem hidden underground. Several measurements must have been taken with the aid of a plumb bob to record the progress of this uneven settling. Eventually, the west front stopped moving, and construction could continue. The master masons and stonemasons should be proud of their work: probably erected between the end of the 1230s and the beginning of the 1240s, the twin towers are still perfectly in plumb. ◆

With the structure complete, the last touches of polychromy are added to the façade. The retrofits continue with the insertion of lateral chapels along the nave after the enlargement of the clerestory.

1245

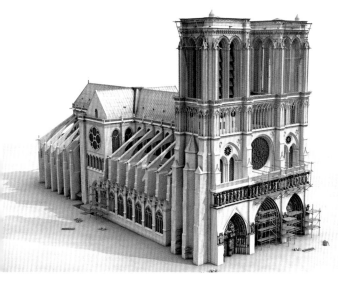

1245

Towers and Bells, Marking Time at the Cathedral

The towers housed the bells, which marked important moments in the day, in people's lives, in the history of the city—and sometimes even of the entire country. Symbolically, liturgists likened the bells to bishops, who watched over the faithful just as the bells structured their lives. Once again, architecture glorified the clergy by materializing its power.

With the construction of these towers, the body of the cathedral was largely complete. These particularly impressive features could be seen from quite a distance in the Parisian landscape, and they were especially important because they housed the voice of the

1. The belfry of the south tower, remade in the nineteenth century, is a structure 25 meters in height that occupies the entirety of the tower above the level of the rose window.

cathedral: its bells. They were first installed only in the north tower, or *grosse tour*—also known as the Guillaume Tower due to the funds allocated to its construction by Bishop Guillaume d'Auvergne (d 1249). It was not until the fifteenth century that the south tower came to house the biggest bells. Still today, the ringing of the bells is inextricably linked with the cathedral, and the largest of them, named Emmanuel, recast under Louis XIV, is justifiably renowned.

The structure of the upper part of the towers was conceived to house the belfries, hidden from view by louvers and from which the bells were suspended **(fig. 1)**. These constructions in wood, roughly 25 meters in height and simply placed on interior indentations in the wall at the level of the openwork gallery, absorbed the pendulum swing of the bells without risking to shake the masonry **(fig. 2)**.

Bells were a part of daily life in the Middle Ages, and it would be hard to overestimate the population's

2. The belfry is simply placed on a masonry recess to prevent the movement caused by the ringing of the bells from shaking the towers.

surprise in their absence, as happened when the clergy, as a means of protest, would suspend religious life. That is exactly what happened for several long months in 1200, during the scandal of the divorce of King Philip II Augustus. Pope Innocent III vigorously condemned the monarch's decision to separate from Queen Ingeborg. The bishop of Paris, Eudes de Sully, followed the pope's orders and put the diocese under interdict, thereby suspending all religious life throughout the diocese. Silencing the bells had consequences well beyond the confines of the cathedral. Rung on many occasions over the course of the day, the bells structured time throughout the city. As a couplet in Latin verse inscribed on a bell at Troyes Cathedral in 1340 and reproduced on the yoke of the Emmanuel bell attested **(fig. 3)**:

> I praise the true God, I call the people, I assemble the clergy
> I mourn the dead, I fend off the plague, I adorn feast days.

Bells were rung at different times of day for religious services, but they also served as markers for economic activities. *The Book of Trades*, by the provost

3. The Emmanuel bell, at 12.8 tons the largest bell of Notre Dame, is the product of several castings (the most recent dating to 1686) in which older bells were used.

1245

Towers and Bells, Marking Time at the Cathedral

of Paris Étienne Boileau, specified around 1260 that the master carpenters had to stop work after the hour of nones was rung by the large bell of Notre Dame: "Que il n'ouverroient au samedi puis que nonne eut sonnée à Nostre-Dame, au gros saint." The bells were also inextricably linked to feast days and other important occasions, joyous or otherwise **(fig. 4)**.

Bell ringing was subject to precise regulations that the churchwardens or bell ringers of Notre Dame had to follow. It was, in fact, one of their primary duties, to the point that their seal featured a representation of a bell, and the clergy made sure to punish them for shirking this responsibility. In fairness to the churchwardens, it must be said that the task was extremely onerous: they had to ring the bells every hour, night and day. The punctuality of bell ringing depended on the regular functioning of two water clocks (clepsydras): one in the cloister, the other in the church. According to fourteenth-century statutes, it was the lay chamberlain who had to keep the clocks filled with water and announce all hours of the day and night ("atremper les horloges, et cheoir et sonner à toutes heures du jour et de la nuit") to indicate to the churchwardens that the time had come

to ring the bells ("l'instant venu de mettre les cloches en branle"). The churchwardens hastened to blame delays in the ringing of the bells on problems with the clocks.

The number of bells that had to be rung simultaneously or in succession required both rigor on the part of the churchwardens and a significant amount of help. The churchwarden had two valets: a cleric who rang the bells in the spire and a layperson who rang the bells in the tower. But due to the weight and number of bells, the latter had to recruit the poor to help him. The jingle of the bells in the spire alerted the lay valet that it was time to ring the bells in the tower. The little bells were struck sixty times, and the large bells were struck fifty, forty, or fewer times. Such groupings were known as *meutes*. The number of strikes increased with the solemnity of the daily office or special ceremony being announced, and also according to the canonical hours. As far as innovations, we might signal the prescription in the *Book of Sermons*, following a copy of the ordinance of 1328, to *cliqueter* (that is, to ring the bell without setting it in motion) while a *Pater* and an *Ave* were recited before signaling curfew. In times of war, ringing bells at night was limited or even eliminated entirely.

The largest bells, known as *bourdons*, were rung continuously only on feast days. Sixteen men were required to set each one into motion, which came at a certain cost, even if the churchwardens recruited

4. Detail of Jean Fouquet, *The Right Hand of God Protecting the Faithful Against the Demons*, illumination from the Hours of Étienne Chevalier, ca. 1452–60 (New York, Metropolitan Museum of Art, Robert Lehman Collection, 1975, ms 12490). Notre Dame dominates the city throughout which its bells resounded.

1245

Towers and Bells, Marking Time at the Cathedral

beggars in order to be able to pay them as little as possible. This practice was cause for recrimination from the clergy, who worried about the disorder that this activity would cause in the upper reaches of the cathedral. This is the origin of the name Tower *des Ribauds*, given to the south tower at the end of the Middle Ages **(fig. 5)**. According to the statutes dating to the beginning of the fourteenth century, the bells were rung from the top of the towers. In 1392, the chapter restricted this practice to daytime bell ringing, with nighttime bell ringing required to take place from below. Nighttime access to the towers was forbidden, due to the risk of fire from going there with a candle or lantern. Since it was more difficult to ring the bells from below than from above, the chapter had to offer additional compensation to the bell ringer. In 1404, access to the belfry was denied, even during the day, and the churchwardens had to return the keys to the towers, with some financial incentive.

Additional services, particularly burials, required special bell ringing, with specific allocations for the churchwardens: 40 *sous* for the funeral of a canon of Notre Dame; 20 *sous* for a canon of Saint-Denis-du-Pas,

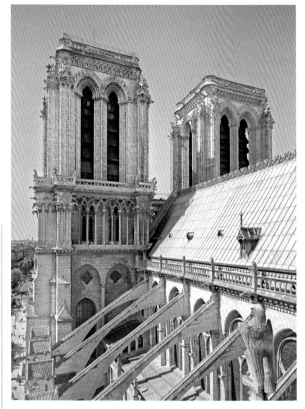

5. The south tower owes its nickname, "Ribalds' Tower," to the fact that it housed a somewhat seedy population of bell ringers.

Saint-Jean-le-Rond, or a vicar. For benefactors' funerals, payment was not mandatory, but generous donations were not out of the question!

While the cathedral must have contained bells from the beginning, they are first documented only in 1198, when Eudes de Sully mentioned the ringing of the bells on the eve of the Feast of Fools (January 6). The composition of the bells of Notre Dame are known from the

6. The north tower, still known as the great tower or the Guillaume tower, was until the early fifteenth century the only one to contain suspended bells.

who was at the head of the Church of Paris between 1117 and 1124. The bell christened Chambellan, first mentioned in the sources in 1283, to indicate that it had been taken down for two years for repair, may have been given by Pierre Sarrazin, Louis IX's chamberlain, who made large donations to the cathedral, where he also endowed a chaplaincy.

The bells required numerous repairs. They could be damaged by excessive or improper use, their wooden racks sometimes collapsing under the weight of the bells and enormous pressure of being rung continuously. Also mentioned are the bells named Pasquier, whose clapper was already broken in 1283; Louis (repaired in 1335–36); and Mary (cast or recast in 1378–79). La Pugnèse was the name given to the principal bell of the spire over the crossing, which contained seven bells. Among them was la Clopette, probably a small handbell.

We still find the same number of bells in the large tower at the end of the fourteenth century. In 1424, no more than four remained. But since around 1400, in the south tower **(fig. 7)**, another large bell was in place, named Jacqueline. The bell derived its name from

beginning of the fourteenth century, at which point there were eight bells in the large tower, or Guillaume Tower—that is, the north tower of the western frontispiece **(fig. 6)**—and six small bells in the spire over the crossing.

The Guillaume bell was donated before 1249 by Bishop Guillaume d'Auvergne, who gave it its name. The Gilbert bell (mentioned when it was repaired in 1335–36) may have been a gift of the bishop by that name

1245

Towers and Bells, Marking Time at the Cathedral

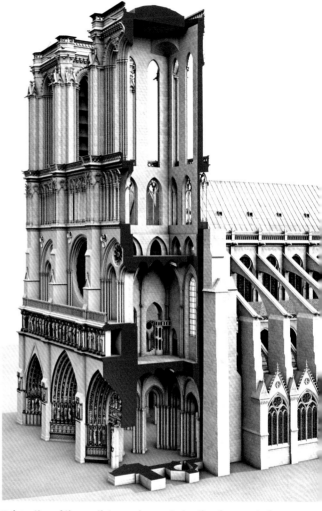

Jacqueline de la Grange, the wife of the donor Jean de Montaigu, the king's butler and brother of Gérard de Montaigu, bishop of Paris from 1409 to 1420. It originally weighed 11,542 pounds. After it was recast in 1686, it weighed 36,000 pounds and was rechristened Emmanuel-Marie-Thérèse: this is the large bourdon of Notre Dame, its only surviving bell that predates the French Revolution. The ringing of the bells of the north tower was restored in 1856, and a bell taken in the Battle of Sevastopol joined the Emmanuel bell until 1913, when it was given back to the Russian Empire. A new suspended bell was installed in the north tower in 2013.

The Casting of a Bell

The complex and highly unstable operation of bell casting exemplifies the challenges confronted by the overseers of the project. They had to solve problems

7. A section of the south tower demonstrates the placement of an upper chapel above the space on the ground level opposite the Saint Anne portal, emptied out to house the belfry.

8. The circular opening in the vault of the upper chapel was added after the fact to allow bells to pass through it.

pragmatically, while ensuring the reuse of as much of the material as possible.

In 1396, the recasting of the bell named Marie took place in the shadow of the cathedral, likely in the small cloister near Saint-Denis-du-Pas, immediately east of the chevet. The clerk of the fabric, Jean de Villiers, subdivided the account into five parts. He referred to the procurement of wood for the required machinery and a hemp rope 62 *toises* in length (around 120 meters) and weighing 400 pounds, imperative for taking down the old bell **(fig. 8)**. He also mentioned the purchase and reuse of metal for the casting itself, as well as the rental, by requisition, of seventeen bellows from the founders of Paris, which included covering the cost of food for the workers and distributing pieces of base metal as payment (more than a hundred workers were required to operate the bellows during the half-day necessary for metal casting). Finally, to this must be added site clean-up—particularly the schools of Saint-Denis-du-Pas, the cloister, and the plaza—where the old bell was melted down and the new one was cast and installed.

These operations, begun at the end of March 1396, were not finished until mid-November. Under the direction of Thomas de l'Hay, official carpenter of the church, Thomas de Claville, a Parisian founder, and the locksmith Thomas de Beauvais, they mobilized crews of workers and numerous other individuals. They used 12,284 pounds of metal: 800 pounds were purchased from the prior of Saint-Martin-des-Champs (likely sourced from an old bell of that church), 793 pounds from one Renaud Morise, of the rue Saint-Martin, and 221 pounds of tin from the spice merchant Jean Testart, of the rue Saint-Denis; 120 pounds came from a small bell in the cathedral spire, 9,350 pounds from the bell Marie itself, and 1,000 pounds from another bell. After the new bell was cast, 2,000 pounds of pure and 60 pounds of impure metal remained, as well as 60 pounds of tin, which was used, in part, to repair the organ and weld the stained glass of the cathedral. The new bell weighed 10,164 pounds (roughly 5 tons) and cost the considerable sum of 410 livres, 16 sous, and 6 deniers to produce. ◆

The transformations to the structure of the cathedral continue with the most spectacular operations: the addition of a lead-covered wooden spire over the crossing and new transept façades fitted with gigantic rose windows. The south rose gives onto the courtyard of the episcopal palace.

1265

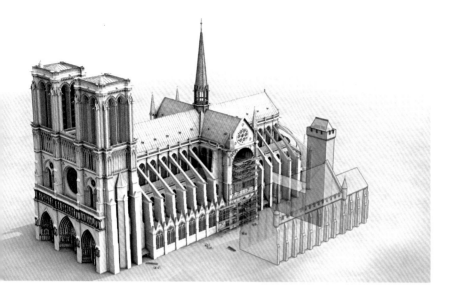

1265

Relics and Processions

Relics and Reliquaries

The prestige of a church is linked to its status, and also to the relics it possesses, the sainted remains of holy figures whose reputation was immediately reflected in the sanctuary that housed them. In Paris and its environs, the cathedral suffered from a cruel irony. The body of its first bishop, Denis, martyred in the third century, rested north of the capital city, in the church of an extremely powerful abbey that took his name, as did the entire surrounding area: Saint-Denis. The body of Saint Germain (d. 576), another sainted bishop of Paris, had been interred in the abbey founded by the Merovingian king Childebert (son of Clovis) at the threshold of Paris on the Left Bank.; Germain was

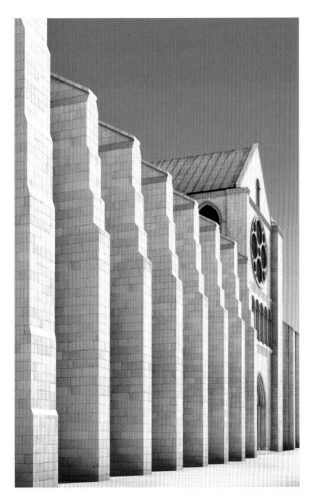

1 and 2. The addition, beginning in the 1220s, of lateral chapels to the flanks of the nave substantially changed the overall appearance of the monument: the rhythmic composition accentuated by a series of projecting buttresses became a nearly flat surface punctuated by enormous windows.

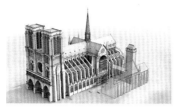

1265

Relics and Processions

present at its consecration in 558, and his name graced the institution beginning in the ninth century. The patron saint of Paris, Genevieve, was venerated at the monastery that Clovis himself had founded at the top of a hill known as Mount Saint Genevieve. In the Middle Ages, the shrine housing that saint had priority over all the other relics in the city, until Louis IX obtained the relics of the Passion of Christ—including the Crown of Thorns—for which he had the Sainte-Chapelle built, completed in 1248.

Bishops and canons of the cathedral made every effort to obtain relics. They collected a large number, which they kept safe on the Île de la Cité during the Norman invasions of the ninth century. It was likely at this time that the body of Saint Marcel (d. 436), bishop of Paris, came into their possession—a figure far less renowned than Saint Denis or Saint Germain **(fig. 3)**. Nevertheless, the cathedral clergy lavished all their efforts on it, even making it their primary relic. A considerable bequest of 1,000 livres, received from the canon Raymond de Clermont when the transept façades were being rebuilt, permitted the relics of Saint Marcel to be translated into a magnificent metalwork shrine realized in the 1260s. This silver gilt reliquary, enhanced with precious and semiprecious stones, was placed in the sanctuary on a platform perched atop four arcades of copper columns, right behind the high altar, overlooking it. The shrine took the form of a three-aisled church six bays in length, its lateral flanks punctuated by buttresses, between which appeared arcades framing representations of the twelve apostles **(fig. 4)**. Bays featuring two lights resembled the clerestory windows of the main vessel of the cathedral itself. One of the gables featured Saint Marcel, mitered and holding a crozier, flanked by

3. The trumeau of the Saint Anne portal depicting Saint Marcel alluded to the presence of the body of the saint—the cathedral's principal relic—in the sanctuary. The bishop is depicted defeating the dragon that had menaced the outskirts of Paris.

4. The shrine of Saint Marcel (in the middle ground) followed immediately behind that of Saint Genevieve (in the foreground) during solemn processions (detail of figure 11, below).

a pair of torch-bearing angels. Scenes illustrating the life of the sainted bishop were inserted on the slopes of the gable roof of the main vessel. The aisle roofs were covered with fleur-de-lis incised within lozenges, with enameled gold simulating glass. The sumptuousness of the shrine astonished Mme de Sévigné when she saw it carried in a procession by the goldsmiths' guild in 1675: "Its stones were worth two million: it was the most beautiful thing in the world." Until the French Revolution, it remained the most important object in the Notre Dame treasury. Its weight, estimated at 436 marks—more than 100 kilograms—made it one of the most imposing Gothic metalwork shrines, more than twice as heavy as the shrine of Saint Genevieve produced by the goldsmith Bonnardus in 1242, which it followed in major processions.

In 1120, the clergy of Notre Dame received an authenticated relic fragment of the True Cross, given

1265

Relics and
Processions

5. The Boucicaut Master, *Procession of the Cross of Anseau*, illumination from the Breviary of the Dauphin Louis de Guyenne, ca. 1414 (Bibliothèque municipale de Châteauroux, ms Fr. 2, fol. 265). The procession with the prestigious relic is about to enter Notre Dame. This illumination is the oldest representation of the portals of the cathedral.

by a former canon, named Anseau, who had become the cantor at the church of the Holy Sepulchre in Jerusalem **(fig. 5)**. This major relic was the most important one linked to the Passion of Christ before the acquisition by Louis IX of the relics of the Passion—including the famous Crown of Thorns—in 1239. It likely inspired the articulation of the oculi of the third story of the choir, adorned with large crosses so delicately worked that they evoked gigantic sumptuous metalwork objects **(fig. 6)**. The repetition of the emblem of the cross in the vault keystones of the choir, transept, aisles, and tribunes of the east end of the nave all likely referred to the same relic in the context of the late twelfth century, when the crusades remained a burning question.

During the construction of the cathedral, an episode linked to the relics had important repercussions.

Contemporary chroniclers reported that in the 1180s, relics were discovered in the church of Saint Stephen, the small church dedicated to that saint on the Left Bank, where they must have been sheltered in the past. King Philip II Augustus returned them to the cathedral, and the clergy created as a solemn feast the ceremony of *Susceptio reliquiarum*, celebrated each year on December 4. Among the relics were a lock of the Virgin Mary's hair, three of John the Baptist's teeth, stones from the Stoning of Saint Stephen, the top of Saint Denis's skull, and an arm of Saint Andrew.

In the following decades, the clergy fixed the number of feasts in direct relation to the possession of relics of saints linked to the diocese of Paris. To codify these liturgical practices, a large number of missals were copied. The polyphonic pieces for which the Notre Dame school is best known were composed largely to increase the liturgical splendor of the feasts in honor of these saints.

At the end of the Middle Ages, the sanctuary housed no fewer than seven reliquary shrines. In addition to

6. Arm of one of the sculpted stone crosses that decorated the oculi of the third level of the original elevation (Musée Carnavalet).

1265

Relics and Processions

that of Saint Marcel, the most sumptuous, there was the silver shrine of Notre Dame, which contained the relics of several saints—those of Saint Lucain, Saints Cosmas and Damian, Saint Justin, Saint Séverin, and Saint Gendulphe, all united at the end of the apse. In addition to the long list of saints of great renown, the inventories attest to the presence of "unknown relics no one dares set eyes on, at the risk of becoming blind!" This passage speaks to the supernatural power attributed to these material witnesses to the lives of the saints. Other relics were stored in the cathedral treasury, located directly to the south of the choir, on the upper level of the passageway that linked the cathedral to the episcopal palace. Items such as the arm-reliquary of Saint Andrew or the head-reliquary of Saint Gendulphe (d. ca. 921–22), bishop of Paris, were displayed on their feast days. Only distinguished visitors, such as princes and prelates, would be shown the relics at other moments, a devotional practice that developed particularly in the late Middle Ages, the clergy taking care to record the gifts given by such important figures as payment for this privilege.

While their relics were only occasionally visible, the saints were familiar to laypeople thanks to numerous representations calling attention to the presence of sacred remains inside the church. It is thus that we can make sense of the depiction on the north portal of the west façade of John the Baptist, Saint Genevieve, and Saint Germain—many of whose liturgical vestments the cathedral possessed—or of Saint Denis carrying his severed head in his hands, a direct reference to the relic claimed by the canons of Notre Dame, provoking the fury of the monks of Saint-Denis, who claimed to possess the entire body of their patron saint. Saint Stephen appeared on the portal of the south transept façade. His martyrdom, rendered in particularly graphic detail, is the subject of the tympanum and relates to the presence in the treasury of stones associated with this event **(fig. 7)**. The depiction of the miracles of Saint Marcel in the voussoirs of the *Porte Rouge* on the north flank of the choir closely resembled those depicted on the roof of his shrine. The refined quality of the sculpture of the base of this portal **(fig. 8)** emulated the metalwork techniques that clearly inspired the treatment of the socles of the statues of the portal of the south transept arm, whose cusped arches were adorned with fleurs-de-lis damaged in the Revolution **(fig. 9)**, a recurring motif on the shrine of Saint Marcel.

7. Stoning of Saint Stephen on the portal of the south arm of the transept of Notre Dame, ca. 1260. The cathedral treasury contained stones associated with the martyrdom.

1265

Relics and Processions

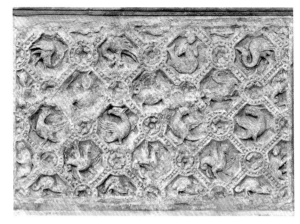

8. Through its delicate treatment, the carving of the lower embrasure of the Porte Rouge evokes the treatment of metalwork reliquaries in the cathedral treasury.

Stational Liturgy and Processions

Since at least the beginning of the thirteenth century, a tradition emerged wherein, on certain feast days, the clergy would leave the liturgical choir at the end of vespers in order to process to a chapel or appear before the statue of the saint whose feast was being celebrated that day **(figs. 1–2)**. After a brief stational service, they would return to the choir chanting an antiphon in praise of the Virgin Mary. In the fourteenth century, it was customary for the station to stop before the statue of the Virgin affixed to the southeast transept pier, where the prosa *Inviolata intacta et casta* was sung, from which the name *statio de inviolata* came to be used to refer to this rite **(fig. 10)**; it benefitted from numerous donations from members of the clergy, such as the 25-pound annuity Bishop Guillaume de Chanac promised in 1350 to ensure that it would be sung during Holy Week.

Certain processions extended well beyond the confines of the cathedral. This was particularly true during Lent; the clergy would process carrying the

9. The lower embrasure of the Saint Stephen portal on the south transept arm retains traces of fleurs-de-lis, picking up a motif documented to have adorned the shrine of Saint Marcel in the sanctuary.

shrine of the Virgin three times each of the five weeks of Lent. Over the course of fifteen processions, they covered virtually all of the territory of Paris and its outskirts. Members of the chapter likewise visited Parisian churches on the feasts of their titular saints; in June and July, for example, they would go by boat to Saint-Paul and Saint-Victor, greeted along the way by the clergy of Saint-Jean-en-Grève and Saint-Gervais. At Saint-Martin-des-Champs, the chapter had the privilege of being able to free robbers imprisoned in the priory. These processions, through which the chapter of Notre Dame affirmed its spiritual authority, illustrated the link between the cathedral and the rest of the churches of the city. In addition to strengthening institutional bonds, the processions likewise allowed the clergy to

10. On the north transept portal, ca. 1250, Theophilus petitions the Virgin Mary for protection before an altar resembling the one against the *jubé* that attracted pious devotions.

1265

Relics and
Processions

mingle with the laity of Parisian parish churches, as well as passersby who assembled in great numbers along the route. The shrine of Saint Marcel was carried in procession on certain occasions, for which the shrine of Saint Genevieve would also be sought out at the eponymous abbey; the two, with Genevieve at the front, followed a fixed route, before the bishop would accompany the patron saint of Paris to the sanctuary. These solemn processions were organized to appease the divine wrath considered to be at the root of various calamities—including natural disasters (floods, droughts) and political and military crises—that proliferated during the Hundred Years' War and beyond **(fig. 11)**.

The processions leading up to the Feast of the Ascension, during the three rogation days, were particularly popular. A large wicker dragon was carried through the streets of Paris over the course of three days. It recalled the man-eating monster Saint Marcel had defeated in the fifth century by passing his stole over the beast's neck. The skeleton of a lizard under the vaults of the church of Saint Marcel was taken to be the skeleton of this monster. Into the gaping mouth

11. Procession toward Notre Dame of the shrines of Saint Genevieve and Saint Marcel, visible near the center of the image, on May 27, 1694. Anonymous engraving, detail (BnF).

of the wicker simulacrum, the crowd would throw fruit and cakes. This folkloric element persisted until the eighteenth century. It is likely that this dragon puppet was created at the end of the twelfth century or at the

12. Saint Marcel subdues the dragon terrorizing Parisians by wrapping his stole around its neck. Voussoir of the Porte Rouge, ca. 1270.

beginning of the thirteenth. It is documented from the beginning of the fourteenth century, as the fabric accounts refer to the costs associated with the replacement of several teeth in the dragon's mouth! Around 1180, the Parisian liturgist John Beleth explained that the dragon represented the Devil, and Jacques de Vitry, a celebrated preacher, referred to this puppet in a sermon about rogation processions: on the first two days, the dragon led the cortege, ahead of the croziers and banners carried by the clergy, its long tail inflated and pointing upward. But on the third day, it was relegated to the back of the procession, its tail deflated and low to the ground. For Jacques de Vitry, this dragon represented the devil, the three rogation days signifying the three ages of the world (the age before the law, the age under the law, and the age of grace). In the first two ages, the devil was dominant, but in the third, after Christ's victory, he would fall from heaven. It thus became a defeated dragon that followed the people pitifully, having lost his ability to inflict harm.

Like the Tarasque of Tarascon, in southern France, the wicker dragon of Notre Dame was likely a kind of emblem of the community, of a homeland the bishop vigorously defended. It was perhaps even an emblem of Paris, even before the red and blue caps or the boat on the Seine—linked to the city's motto, *Fluctuat nec mergitur*—were instituted, encouraged by Étienne Marcel, provost of the merchants. ◆

The transformations to Notre Dame continue with the construction of chapels along the perimeter of the choir.

1300

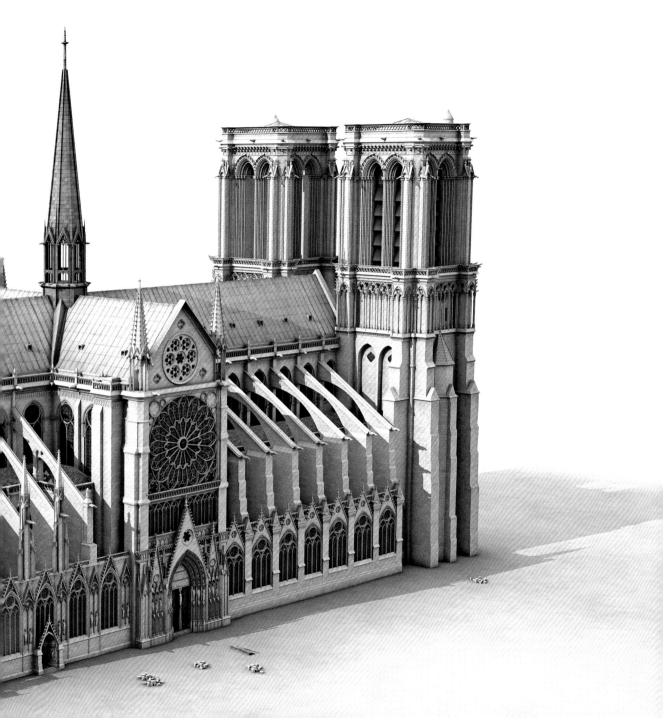

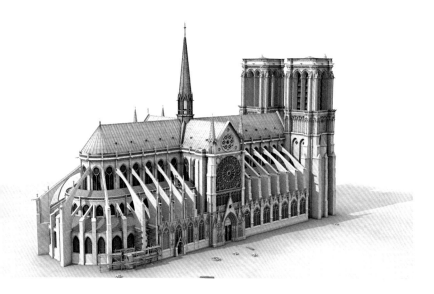

1300

Pious Foundations and Tombs

In a society preoccupied to the point of obsession with eternal salvation, represented effectively in the center portal **(figs. 8–9)** as well as on the *jubé* **(fig. 3)**, the dead had an important place. Eminent episcopal and capitular figures were commemorated at the cathedral, and chaplains prayed for the salvation of the donors who had enriched the church with pious foundations. Their names were carefully preserved in the necrology on their death date, in the belief that the prayers or "suffrages" of future generations would aid in the salvation of their souls. Thus arose at the end of the Middle Ages the foundation of commemorative masses, the most solemn of which was celebrated at the high altar, and the rest at the altars of the various chapels distributed throughout the building. Effigies of the founders proliferated, with a precise geographic distribution that reserved the choir and the sanctuary for the bishops and certain princes, authorized clerical foundations in the nave, ambulatory, and chapels, and, until the fifteenth century, proved rather strict with respect to lay burials.

1. On the south transept portal, the burial of Saint Stephen (ca. 1260) takes the form of a Christian burial overseen by a priest and his acolytes.

Thus, in life as in death, the cathedral remained the preserve of the elite.

The Choir: Preserve of Prelates and Princes

From the beginning of the thirteenth century, Notre Dame became the primary episcopal necropolis, supplanting abbeys such as Saint-Victor, which had housed the tombs of several twelfth-century bishops, including that of the prelate who initiated the project for the Gothic cathedral, Maurice de Sully (d. 1196).

Positioned between the choir stalls, beneath the keystone of the vault of the first double bay of the choir, the tomb of Eudes de Sully (d. 1208), the first bishop to be inhumed in the Gothic cathedral, received special treatment **(fig. 2)**: the thick bronze slab from which the figure of the bishop emerged in relief, flanked by

2. Bronze tomb of Eudes de Sully, the first bishop to be buried in the cathedral in 1208 (seventeenth-century drawing, Gaignières collection, BnF).

1300

Pious Foundations and Tombs

3. Late medieval laypeople favored interpreting this grimacing mask in flames from the *jubé* of Notre Dame, ca. 1230, as a likeness of Pierre de Cugnière, advisor to King Philip VI, eternally punished for taking a stand against the privileges of the Church, a myth the clergy did nothing to dispel (Louvre, département des Sculptures).

two censing angels, was, rather unusually, signed by its creator, Étienne de Boisses. Until the eighteenth century, it remained visible to the celebrants charged with praying for the bishop's salvation. The tombs of other bishops were located nearby: the stone tombs of Barthélemy (d. 1227) and Gauthier de Château-Thierry (d. 1249), and the copper-alloy tombs of Hugues de Besançon (d. 1332) and Pierre de Bellperche. While never bishop of Paris, the latter had been dean of the Paris cathedral chapter before his election as bishop of Auxerre, where he died in 1308. Within the sanctuary or in close proximity to it were located, on the privileged Gospel side—that is, on the left, or north, side—the tombs of Pierre de Nemours (d. 1219), Étienne Tempier (d. 1279), Aimery de Maignac (d. 1385), and Pierre d'Orgemont (d. 1409) against the first bay of the arcade on the north side of the apse. All of these tombs were made of copper alloy, except the last, realized in marble.

On the orders of Philip II Augustus, the princely tomb of Geoffroy, count of Brittany, entered the choir shortly after the completion of that part of the building. The king wanted to proclaim his closeness to his ally, who died unexpectedly in Paris in 1186. The king's first

wife, Isabelle of Hainaut, was likewise buried there in 1190, according to her last wishes. The sepulcher of the eldest son of Louis VIII and Blanche of Castile, Philip, who died prematurely in 1218, was also placed in the choir. But one of the very first people to be buried in the choir was the brother of Louis VII, Philip, who died in 1161. This figure from the royal line was closely linked to Notre Dame due to his ecclesiastical career there, notably as archdeacon. However, he was denied the episcopal throne in favor of his teacher, the theologian Peter Lombard.

The cathedral choir housed some princely tombs from the twelfth century and numerous ecclesiastical tombs (which increased in number until the end of the Middle Ages). This was one way to demonstrate the close links between the cathedral clergy and the crown. It was also in the sanctuary that a representation of Philip II Augustus was placed, a few years at most after the end of his reign in 1223. Removed in the seventeenth century, it celebrated the king as protector of the Church and founder of religious services in the cathedral, but also as the victor of the Battle of Bouvines, which earned him the epithet "Augustus."

From the mid-thirteenth century, the canons, until then buried largely in the cloister northeast of the cathedral, now began to have their tombs placed in the nave of the great church, as well as in the lateral chapels added in the same period. The large sculpted tombstone of the canon Étienne Yver (d. 1468), located in the last lateral chapel on the north side of the nave, is a fine example of late medieval funerary art **(fig. 4)**.

4. Tombstone of Canon Étienne Yver (d. 1468). Above the "transi" representation of the dead as a decomposing body appears his resurrection at the end of time, accompanied by Saint John and Saint Stephen, under Christ of the Apocalypse.

1300

Pious Foundations and Tombs

The Chapels

Beginning at the end of the twelfth century, chapels whose founders ensured that the chaplains received a stipend were added to Notre Dame. Commemorative masses were celebrated in these chapels for the departed patrons—mostly members of the clergy but eventually also wealthy laypeople. In the Middle Ages, the term "chapel" usually referred to a religious foundation as opposed to the place where such foundations were celebrated. The proliferation of altars, which risked encumbering the interior, led to the construction of aedicules between the lateral buttresses, first in the nave, and then in the choir. This ingenious intervention consisted of integrating into the church interior space that had once been outside between the uprights of the flying buttresses; by moving the lateral wall of the outer aisle outward, the perimeter of the building was now flush with the uprights of the flying buttresses. Quadripartite rib vaults were added to cover the new chapels. This expansion took place over the course of less than a century. Visual analysis of the architecture suggests a date around 1225–35 for the oldest chapels—that is, the first four on the north side of the nave. The lateral chapels on the south side of the nave, for which we have three references to foundations of chaplaincies between 1236 and 1241, were built shortly thereafter. The last three chapels on the north side of the nave were constructed around 1250.

5 and 6. The wall that enclosed the aisles in the twelfth century with single lancet windows was suppressed in the thirteenth century with the construction of lateral chapels that brought about the enlargement of the interior space at ground level.

Only two foundations specifically mention the construction of a chapel. The first was dedicated to Saint John the Baptist and Mary Magdalene, the fourth on the north flank of the choir, for which the canon Gilbert de Saana gave an annuity of 14 Parisian livres in 1288, as well as a gift of 100 livres *tournois* for the construction of the chapel. The foundation of Bishop Simon de Bucy in 1296 involved the three-bay axial chapel containing three altars originally dedicated to Saint Rigobert, Saint Marcel, and Saint Nicaise **(figs. 5–6)**.

The prelate gave 600 livres *tournois* for the chaplaincy and 200 for the construction of the chapel. It was there that he chose to be buried; his white marble tomb effigy, now in the ambulatory, was placed against the right wall of the chapel, underneath a monumental painting representing the Virgin Mary, patron saint of the cathedral, flanked by Saints Denis and Nicaise. This painting, heavily restored in the nineteenth century, is a rare remaining trace of such lavish episcopal foundations. The chapter had a kneeling statue of the bishop placed at

1300

Pious Foundations and Tombs

7. The Jouvenal des Ursins family, between 1445 and 1449 (Musée de Cluny). This large family of eleven children founded a chapel at Notre Dame, in which sculptures of the parents praying remain.

the entrance to the chapel. Its socle, still extant, features an inscription attesting to the foundation and the generosity Simon de Bucy exhibited toward his church.

A series of screens isolated the chapels from the rest of the church to prevent the theft of the liturgical furnishings kept there in chests. The altars were originally placed against the east wall of the chapels, echoing the placement of the high altar of the cathedral.

Low masses celebrated at the secondary altars in the chapels were not to interfere with the High Mass at the high altar. From 1209, the chanting of the chaplains, in a high or low voice, was regulated. Several chaplains might succeed one another throughout the day at the same altar, since a single chapel could be endowed with numerous chaplaincies. By the end of the Middle Ages, an average of five chaplains per altar celebrated roughly 120 daily masses at the cathedral.

Confraternities at Notre Dame

Whereas members of the cathedral clergy and the nobility could make individual foundations **(fig. 7)**, members of the bourgeoisie largely made collective foundations through confraternities, the spiritual arm of the guilds and commercial associations. Pious institutions administered by members united by a profession or artisanal craft existed well before the Gothic cathedral was built. A confraternity or association of the Twelve Apostles is already attested at Notre Dame around the turn of the tenth century. Another group was established in the twelfth century in honor of the famous *miracle des ardents* of 1128. From the thirteenth century, the *"Confraternitas Beatae Mariae Parisiensis surgentium ad matutinas"* brought together clerics and other devout people living in or near the cathedral cloister; they joined the cathedral clergy at midnight to celebrate the office of matins.

It was not until the end of the fourteenth century that a confraternity of artisans was permitted to

operate at the cathedral. It was the confraternity of the shoemakers, which joined the master cobblers in 1393–94 in the chapel dedicated to Saints Crépin and Crépinien on the south side of the nave. Such groups proliferated in the fifteenth century with the confraternity of the archers of Paris in the Saint Sebastian chapel (1434), that of the goldsmiths in the Saint Anne chapel (1449), and that of the city barbers at the altar *des ardents* (1475). These institutions celebrated, in a low voice, daily requiem masses in their respective chapels. On the feast day of their patron saint, they would celebrate a solemn mass, likewise at the chapel's altar. Attempts on the part of the confraternities to move these celebrations to the high altar were always

8. Scene of hell in the center portal, ca. 1230. Sexual transgressions, including those by kings and clerics, are depicted with great expressivity in order to discourage the faithful from the temptation to sin.

1300
Pious Foundations and Tombs

9. The elect in heaven are recognizable by their crowns: they form a serene crowd, perfectly ordered, in opposition to the tumult of hell.

thwarted by the chapter, who refused to allow these devotions to take place in the choir or sanctuary. From the time of its foundation in 1474, the confraternity of candle merchants was installed in Saint-Jean-le-Rond. But unlike southern European confraternities, which conducted sumptuous services, those of Notre Dame remained relatively discreet. Far from being deliberate on the part of the members of the confraternities themselves, the cathedral chapter imposed this modesty, careful to reserve such liturgical and musical splendor for itself. In the late Middle Ages, ex-votos became increasingly common, offered to make good on a vow or to give thanks to a saint or the Virgin Mary, whom the donor credited with the positive resolution of a problem. It was in this vein that a painted wood equestrian statue of Philip the Fair in a gesture of thanksgiving was placed against the southwest crossing pier

following his victory against the Flemish at the Battle of Mons-en-Pévèle (1304), which he attributed to the intervention of the Virgin **(fig. 10)**. This representation, facing the statue of the Virgin Mary attached to the *jubé* placed the king, as it were, at the head of the faithful. Other figures populated the cathedral as a reminder of their pious donations, like the wax statues of Pope Gregory XI (1370–78), former canon of Notre Dame, accompanied by his niece and nephew. These representations, situated opposite the same altar of the Virgin Mary—known as *Immacolata*—where Gregory XI had

10. Ex-voto of King Philip the Fair (1304), against the southwest crossing pier, facing the altar of the Virgin (seventeenth-century drawing, Gaignières collection, BnF).

11. At the other end of the nave, a colossal statue of Saint Christopher greeted the faithful from the early fifteenth century until its demolition in the eighteenth century (eighteenth-century drawing, BnF).

founded a mass, were realized in a fragile material and turned to dust by 1599.

One of the oldest depictions of a layperson inside the cathedral, dating to the beginning of the fifteenth century, was that of Antoine des Essarts. Depicted kneeling atop a column against the first pier on the south side of the nave, the man, recently ennobled, belonged to an important Parisian family. Deeply ensconced in the political vicissitudes of the day, he attributed his release from prison at the time of the Cabochien revolt of 1413 to the miraculous intervention of Saint Christopher.

He had a colossal ex-voto statue of the saint, roughly 9 meters in height, placed against the second pier on the south side of the nave of Notre Dame **(fig. 11)**. Though sixteenth-century visitors still admired the statue and were amazed by its scale, it fell out of fashion in the eighteenth century. The chapter removed it in 1786, citing damage inflicted on the statue following work performed nearby, during a period that saw the removal of many monuments of this kind, as well as countless tombstones that had formed the cathedral's pavement since the Middle Ages. ◆

The finishing touches to Notre Dame are complete: the jubé forms a carefully crafted enclosure at the west end of the choir, and the gables, accented with color, articulate the entrances to the ambulatory. Wall painting in a combination of ochre and white throughout the building renders the stained glass more legible.

1350

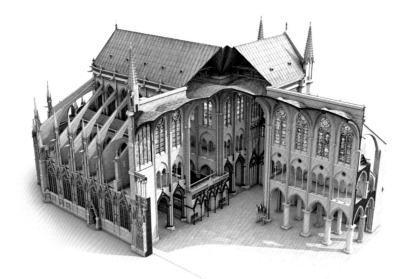

1350
A Point of Reference

1. Inscription *in situ* commemorating the beginning of construction on the south transept façade on February 12, 1258, by the architect Jean de Chelles.

The construction of Notre Dame was a collective effort whose contributors, as we saw in the second chapter, remained anonymous until the mid-thirteenth century. From that point on, the names of some architects renowned for their talent are documented, and the repeated appearance of certain family names suggests the existence of veritable dynasties. This was common for medieval building sites, which became preferred areas for training numerous groups of tradespeople working there. The architect, or master mason, was at the head of a group of artisans with varying skill levels, subject to the resources of the fabric as well as the scale and the urgency of the work. The accounts of the fabric, the organization under the chapter's control charged with financing and overseeing the project, survive, in part, beginning in 1333. They illustrate clearly the irregular pace at which the work unfolded, at a point when the body of the building was long since complete but its daily maintenance and repairs, occasionally major, occupied the attention of the workers who remained on site, close to the lodge that protected them from the elements.

Notre Dame was—as it was for theological and musical instruction—an excellent training ground for the building trades, judging by the renown of its architects: beginning in the fourteenth century, they frequently held the titles of royal architect or architect of the city of Paris.

The Architects

After the construction of the main structure, where the intervention of several master masons is only discernible through architectural analysis, beginning in the mid-thirteenth century, men of enormous prestige directed the building project. The first, Jean de Chelles, is named in an inscription at the base of the thirteenth-century south transept façade **(fig. 1)**: "In the year of grace 1257, on February 12, this was begun in honor of the mother of Christ by Master Jean de Chelles, a mason during his lifetime." Based on this inscription, it seems likely that Jean de Chelles, to whom this is the only reference, died on this date (actually in 1258; the calendar year began on Easter in medieval Paris), and

1350

A Point of Reference

that he had begun the new south transept façade. Both the care that went into making this inscription and its placement in the well-trafficked courtyard of the episcopal palace imply the level of respect enjoyed by the figure architectural historians credit with the construction of the north transept façade **(figs. 2–3)**. At the height of the north rose window, the individuated head of a male corbel figure at the springing of the vaults may represent the master mason himself **(fig. 8)**. The inscription at the base of the south transept façade could only have been installed with the permission of the religious authorities, but Jean de Chelles's successor, Pierre de Montreuil, may have also played a role in this decision.

The latter mason is recorded as having been the master mason of Notre Dame in 1265, and this building project marked the height of his career before his death in 1267. Pierre de Montreuil completed the south transept façade **(fig. 4)**; there we find his highly linear style, exemplified by the linkage between one level of the

2. North transept portal, ca. 1250. Jean de Chelles was responsible for its particularly novel composition, which takes the form of a polyptych.

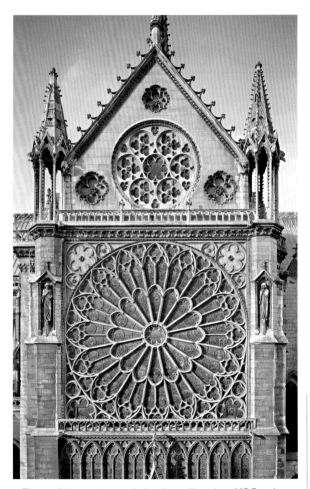

3. The north transept rose window has a diameter of 13.5 meters, a record at the time of its construction in the thirteenth century.

4. The south transept façade, begun by Jean de Chelles and completed by Pierre de Montreuil, who designed the rose window, quite original in its interlocking forms.

elevation and another. These characteristics are to be found in his other buildings, including the Lady Chapel of Saint-Germain-des-Prés, built around 1245–55, only fragments of which survive.

The monks of Saint-Germain must have held him in very high esteem, as they allowed him to be buried there next to his wife. The epitaph on the tomb, a drawing of

1350
A Point of Reference

5. The arcade surmounted by gables by Pierre de Chelles—heavily restored—punctuates the entry to the ambulatory.

which was made prior to its destruction, celebrated the architect in the following manner: "Flower blooming with virtue, in his life doctor of the masons, here lies Pierre, born in Montreuil."

Honored with the title of doctor in architecture, a discipline not taught at university at the time, Pierre was thus elevated to the level of the greatest intellectuals. We know that he also worked at the abbey church of Saint-Denis, and that he owned stone quarries and several houses: he was thus at once an architect and a contractor, and he lived a life of some comfort.

In the first half of the fourteenth century, the master mason of Notre Dame was Pierre de Chelles **(fig. 5)**, probably a relative of Jean de Chelles, who supervised the construction of most of the radiating chapels of the cathedral. Jean Ravy replaced Pierre de Chelles in 1318, continuing the construction of the choir chapels and beginning the choir screen. He enjoyed the unusual privilege of having his likeness depicted on the surface

of the choir screen, near the door inserted into the fifth bay of the choir on the north side **(fig. 6)**. Its inscription read, "This is Master Jehan Ravy, who was mason of Notre Dame of Paris for twenty-six years and began these new sculptures, and Master Jehan le Bouteiller, his nephew, perfected them in the year 1351." It was, it seems, his nephew Jean le Bouteiller who succeeded

6. The sculpted effigy of the architect Jean Ravy (d. 1344) adorned the choir screen realized, in part, through his efforts (BnF).

him in his role to complete the monumental envelope surrounding the liturgical choir.

Taking over the role of master mason in 1363, Raymond du Temple best encapsulates the high profile of the architect: he acquired the most prestigious titles of master mason of Notre Dame and master of the king's works. In addition to offering his professional opinion on the maintenance and repair of buildings throughout the kingdom, he was also responsible for the major retrofit of the Louvre palace under Charles V; the start of the construction of the Sainte-Chapelle of Vincennes, built beginning in 1379 within the walls of the palace (probably designed by the same architect); the collège de Beauvais, the chapel of which remains in the fifth arrondissement; and the construction of the oratory

7. Flying buttresses, south side of the choir. Raymond du Temple redid some of the pinnacles on the uprights of the flying buttresses in the last third of the fourteenth century before they were replaced yet again in the nineteenth century.

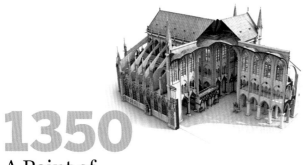

1350

A Point of Reference

added to the south flank of the Sainte-Chapelle linked to the palace on the Île de la Cité.

The work of Raymond du Temple at Notre Dame itself largely involved maintenance, with some significant repairs: the recreation of the pinnacles of the buttressing system **(fig. 7)** and the substitution of a parapet for the timber-framed roofs of the ambulatory. He reconstructed the Saint Thomas chapel of the Hôtel-Dieu, opposite the Saint Anne portal of the cathedral. The chapter authorized him to live with his family in the canons' cloister. He insisted that one of his sons, Jean, succeed him, which occurred after his death in 1405.

Directing the Works

The construction and retrofitting of a building as large as the Gothic cathedral relied upon the efforts of numerous specialized artisans from all of the building trades, working individually or in teams under the direction of the master mason. Fragments of fabric accounts dating to the fourteenth century, as lacunar and laconic as they are, allow us to perceive the continuation

of semipermanent activity at the site, brought about by necessary structural maintenance and updating the style of the building and its decoration. At certain moments, several dozen workers operated within a hierarchical structure, where, apart from certain holidays, work continued during the six workdays of the week. Working on Sunday, theoretically prohibited, occasioned compensation in kind, like the wine offered as payment in 1381–82 to the workers active that day.

We encounter the names of famous artists who were not always hired to perform major works but who might be solicited for modest repairs. The variety of different activities suggests exchanges between one domain and the other at a time when many workers were multiskilled. What we already noted about the architects was likewise true for painters, who might play a role in completing a sculptural ensemble. This did not exclude the possibility of tapping the finest specialists to work in a particular medium, or for prestigious commissions, as was the case for metalwork—the longest chapter of expenses—linked to the retrofits of the sanctuary of the cathedral, which underwent a complete renovation in the fourteenth century.

Under the direction of Raymond du Temple, Jean d'Orléans refurbished five angels surrounding the high altar in 1371 **(figs. 9–10)**. He was no less than the king's painter, who also worked for the dukes of Berry and

8. At the end of the north transept arm, a console depicts the bust of a layperson, possibly a depiction of Jean de Chelles admiring his masterpiece: the great rose window.

1350

A Point of Reference

Burgundy, and he saw to it that his son would take over the role of royal painter in 1407. He himself was the son of Girard d'Orléans, whom he succeeded in this role in 1361. Having made a large donation of 20 florins to the cathedral fabric, Girard most likely worked on this monument, to which he was apparently particularly attached. Thus, like the role of master mason, the work of the painter hints at the accumulation of several prestigious roles: responsibilities at Notre Dame were often conferred upon those who performed similar duties at the court. Moreover, Jean d'Orléans appears at the top of a list containing twenty-five names of painters and five names of image-makers, recorded in 1391 on the occasion of a reform of the trade.

And yet the vast majority of the workers remain anonymous. This varied outfit of masons, carpenters, smiths, glaziers, and so on had a lodge where they kept their tools and that also afforded them the possibility to work sheltered from the elements, with a forge located nearby. The lodge is first mentioned in 1283 in the context of a conflict between the chapter, which had jurisdiction over it, and the bishop's officers. On the eve of the Feast of the Assumption, the latter had unjustly seized some arms—two swords, two knives, and a shield—stored in the lodge. In the fourteenth century, the fabric accounts frequently refer to works of sculpture performed in the lodge, which must have been a site of intense activity. We can only say for certain that it was located from the beginning near Saint-Denis-du-Pas, within the walls of the canons' quarter, at the east end of the cathedral, where the casting of the Mary bell occurred in 1396.

As the principal master working at the site, the architect oversaw the project. The master mason led the teams attached to the masonry and carpentry work as well as the subtrades. The accumulation of duties prevented him from always being present on site, whose continuity he had to ensure. The term *appareilleur* first appears at the end of the thirteenth century to designate an assistant to the architect who was on site permanently. *The Book of Stonecutting of Paris* mentions in 1292 one "mestre Pierre l'appareilleur" who lived on the Île de la Cité, near the chevet of the church of Saint Christopher, a few meters from the cathedral whose construction he may have overseen. Based on the plans of the architect, the *appareilleur* had to create models (*molles*), mostly in wood, for the carpenters and stonecutters who used them as templates for the materials they would use in the planned work. It seems likely that the *appareilleur* exercised authority over the stonecutters on site, because he provided them with models he realized himself. At the end of the thirteenth century, these skills were even more important, since the technical aspects of architecture had become more complex

9 and 10. In the late Middle Ages, the polychromy of the choir highlighted the structural elements (piers and colonnettes), painted in white. The early fourteenth-century replacement of the original, colorful stained glass with lighter glass that made greater use of white glass simultaneously offered greater comfort during the celebration of the liturgy and made the refinement of the new sanctuary furnishings more visible.

in the clever play of forces and balance, as well as in the plastic expression of the different elements—piers, tracery, and moldings. It is easy to fathom that the form of the phalanx of choir flying buttresses with a span of more than 15 meters required competencies of the highest order. The same applied to the design of the window tracery, or the stereotomy of the pinnacles of the uprights of the choir flying buttresses.

The cathedral thus remained a site of constant contact and exchange between workers, artisans, and artists as well as between patrons, architects, and their crews. ◆

In a cathedral with entirely white-washed walls and clear glass, emphasis is placed on the jubé, totally reworked with various types of marble, and the large paintings hanging above the piers in both the nave and the choir.

1780

1780
Baroque Transformations

1. Jean-Baptiste Jouvenet, *The Mass of Canon de La Porte*, 1709 (Musée du Louvre). The canon was one of the main contributors to the retrofit of the cathedral choir in the early eighteenth century. We see him here celebrating Mass at the high altar.

2. The Virgin in bronze by Pierre-Louis Fixon comes from the doors Souf-flot added ca. 1778 (tribunes of Notre Dame).

After a period of intense activity—from around 1160 until the mid-fourteenth century—during which construction continued uninterrupted, work on Notre Dame all but ceased. The building remained relatively unchanged during the following three centuries, even as, all around it, the urban fabric and a string of Parisian parish churches were rebuilt. The clergy, focused on maintaining tradition, apparently considered the cathedral immutable, as it was the monumental setting for the liturgy. It was not until the elevation of Paris from bishopric to archbishopric in 1622 that some remodeling occurred; at that point, a clear royal intervention took place, a sign of the continuation of the alliance between Church and crown, and the greatest architects of the day were solicited. The first works undertaken during this period stemmed from royal patronage, such as the reworking of the altar of the Virgin against the *jubé*, near the southeast crossing pier, which Queen Anne of Austria commissioned from

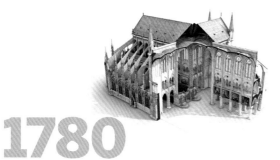

1780

Baroque Transformations

François Mansart in 1628. The architect designed an altar with columns sheltering a Virgin and Child under a dome in its central niche, flanked by Saint Anne and Saint Louis, patron saints of the royal couple. It was the first monument in the cathedral to break with the Gothic style. Ten years later, Louis XIII made a decision even more significant for Notre Dame. In the hopes of having an heir (for which he had long waited in vain) and at a difficult crossroads for the kingdom, at war with Spain, the king, by letters patent drawn up on February 10, 1638, solemnly placed his kingdom and the crown under the protection of the Virgin Mary: this is what is known as the Vow of Louis XIII **(fig. 1)**. Fervent devotion to the Virgin Mary explains the donation, by the canon Michel Le Masle (a close associate of Richelieu), of a cycle of fourteen paintings illustrating the Life of the Virgin, realized between 1640 and 1657, to be placed in the choir. It was sold in 1739 to Strasbourg Cathedral, following the retrofit of the choir of Paris to which they were no longer suited.

Louis XIV renewed his father's vow in 1650. More than ever, Notre Dame was linked to his reign. The vaults resounded with the Te Deums, with organ accompaniment, celebrated to mark the king's victories. Enemy flags seized during battle were hung in the nave: due to

the number of trophies he brought back, the marshal of Luxembourg earned the epithet "tapestry-maker of Notre Dame." Sumptuous funerals, with spectacular scenic designs, were organized in the cathedral choir, ornamented by the most eminent decorators; for example, Jean Bérain transformed the choir in which gigantic catafalques were placed for the likes of the Grand Condé, Louis II de Bourbon (1687), or the duke of Burgundy (1712). Announced in 1638, the restoration of the choir of Notre Dame was not begun until the end of the century at the initiative of Louis XIV, as the royal building projects of the Invalides and the royal chapel at Versailles were under construction. In 1699, the king's chief architect, Jules Hardouin-Mansart, made a drawing for a high altar positioned under a baldachin supported by four spiral columns, in the style of the Counter-Reformation, exemplified in Paris at Val-de-Grâce and the Invalides. This colossal project did not come to fruition right away, and it took a decade for work to get underway. After Hardouin-Mansart died, his brother-in-law Robert de Cotte took over the project. The majority of the work was performed between 1708 and 1714, and the rest was finished by 1723 **(fig. 3)**. It marks an important step in the history of eighteenth-century renovations of cathedral choirs. While he rejected the baldachin of the initial

3. The sculptural representation of the Vow of Louis XIII, spared from revolutionary vandalism, had to form an ensemble with the neo-Gothic altar before a modern cross.

proposal, Robert de Cotte kept Hardouin-Mansart's project for a crypt that would serve as a burial chamber for the archbishops, the excavation for which led to the discovery of remnants of Gallo-Roman sculpture, such as the famous Pillar of the Boatmen (*pilier des Nautes*) now in the Musée de Cluny. In the apse, the medieval stone choir screen was removed in favor of a gilded forged-iron grille featuring the French coat of arms. The columns of the hemicycle were covered with panels of colored marble, and the pointed arches were transformed into round arches. Gilded bronze trophy bases adorned the piers, and the extrados of the arcades were decorated with pairs of reclining Virtues. The medieval pavement and funerary monuments were removed to make way for a new pavement in polychromatic marble, realized in 1712 by the marble-worker Claude Mangeot based on drawings by Jean-Baptiste Blin de Fontenay.

In the sanctuary, raised two steps, the high altar was pushed back against the axial bay of the hemicycle. The marble *Pietà* by Nicolas Coustou, designed in 1712

1780

Baroque Transformations

and realized in 1725, was placed in the central arch of the hemicycle. Guillaume Coustou, his youngest brother, was commissioned to produce the statue of Louis XIII offering his scepter and crown. Its pendant was the statue of Louis XIV in prayer, made by Antoine Coysevox. The two sovereigns, wearing their coronation robes, humbly bowing to the Virgin Mary, followed along the same lines as the statue of Philip II Augustus, which, since the thirteenth century, had watched over the cathedral choir. Six statues of angels bearing the Instruments of the Passion affixed to the marble-clad hemicycle piers accompanied the two angels placed at the high altar.

The liturgical choir, limited to the first four bays of the choir, was refurnished **(fig. 4)**. Robert de Cotte designed two rows of sculpted oak choir stalls, with two large episcopal thrones placed at the end closest to the altar. Above were placed twenty-eight oak panels, left their natural color and alternating between ovals and rectangles, illustrating the Life of the Virgin **(fig. 5)**. Almost certainly designed by René Charpentier, these works, prepared and installed by the woodworkers Jean

4. The early eighteenth-century choir stalls by Robert de Cotte are largely preserved in the current choir.

Noël and Louis Marteau, were realized between 1710 and 1714 by Jules Desgoullons, Pierre Taupin, André Le Goupil, and Robert de Lalande. Above the choir stalls, eight large paintings likewise representing Marian scenes, each more than 4 meters across, obscured the upper part of the arcades and reached the base of the tribunes. The transformed choir of Notre Dame manifested with renewed vigor the alliance between the Church and the crown. The substitution of grillwork

5. Large medallions, alternating between ovals and rectangles, illustrate scenes from the Life of the Virgin.

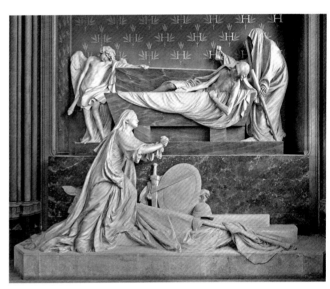

6. Tomb of the count of Harcourt, lieutenant general of the king's armies (1703–1769), by Jean-Baptiste Pigalle. It is one of the most spectacular tombs in the cathedral, a Baroque death scene with the count's widow (who commissioned the work) kneeling in the foreground.

around the hemicycle and the installation of a large transparent gate in place of the medieval *jubé*—between the two lateral altars reconstructed for the occasion by Robert de Cotte (1715)—made the program more visible to laypeople, who were only permitted in the nave, transept, and ambulatory. The rest of the monument remained mostly Gothic, and the contrast was therefore much starker between the choir and sanctuary, on the one hand, and the rest of the building, on the other.

The retrofitting of the choir chapels followed along the same lines, like the chapels Archbishop de Noailles (1695–1729) commissioned from Germain Boffrand in 1708 for his chapel occupying two existing chapels on the north side of the ambulatory, opposite the Saint Remi chapel, which housed the tomb of the count of Harcourt **(fig. 6)**.

1780

Baroque Transformations

This period saw the end of the series of "mays de Notre-Dame" with the suppression of the goldsmiths' confraternity. Since the mid-fifteenth century, they had the habit of making a donation each year in honor of the Virgin Mary. These offerings first took the form of a tree, or "may-verdoyant," and later a tabernacle from which they hung poems before suspending the whole apparatus near the door to the choir. At the beginning of the seventeenth century, a painting replaced the tabernacle, and, as such, between 1630 and 1708, large canvases were commissioned from the most important painters of the day (e.g. Simon Vouet, Sébastien Bourdon, Charles Le Brun). They were placed in the nave against the main arcades or else in the chapels. The desire to bring light into the interior of the cathedral brought about the removal of a great deal of the medieval stained glass, replaced by white glass with a border featuring coats of arms. The master glazier Le Vieil performed this work, leaving untouched only the glass of the three large rose windows. The walls of the cathedral were completely whitewashed a few years before the Revolution, in 1780, under the direction of Jean-Baptiste-Vincent Boulland, the architect of the cathedral chapter. Two Italian painters, Pierre Cietty and Jean-Baptiste Alleman, realized

this work over the course of two and a half months. With the aid of flying scaffolding, attached to the framework of the main roof by ropes passed through holes piercing the vaults, they painted the walls and vaults with tempera the "color of soft stone," in the ring of chapels in the choir and ambulatory, previously whitened in 1777 **(figs. 10–11)**. This operation was controversial. Louis-Sébastien Mercier, attentive to the image of the city in his *Painting of Paris* (1782), expressed his dismay: "This temple . . . lost its venerable color and its imposing darkness that had commanded fervent respect."

To these retrofits, each of which obscured the medieval cathedral a bit more, should be added the more invasive operations that truly damaged it. For example, the center portal of the western frontispiece was robbed of its trumeau and the central portion of the two lintels above, to enable the passage of the canopy for the processions of the Holy Sacrament **(figs. 2 and 7)**. It was the architect Jacques-Germain Soufflot, the author of the Panthéon—upon whom the archbishop had already conferred the construction of a new sacristy (1756–60) **(fig. 8)**—who executed these works in 1771, when some liturgical practices had become incompatible with the medieval structure. Several years later, the architect of the chapter, Jean-Baptiste-Vincent Boulland, was ordered to eliminate the decoration of the south side of the nave, which he replaced with a

7. This engraving, based on a daguerreotype from the first half of the nineteenth century, shows the center portal transformed by Soufflot, who removed the medieval trumeau and cut an arch into the lintels to allow the canopy of the Holy Sacrament to pass through the doors (BnF).

8. Between the cathedral and the episcopal palace of Maurice de Sully, Soufflot built a new sacristy in 1771 (Musée Carnavalet).

flat wall composed of tiles affixed to the masonry using iron dowels. They quickly began to oxidize, eroding the stone to which they were attached. In 1787, a certain Parvy was tapped to remove the stone elements protruding from the building, particularly the crockets and the gargoyles, in order to prevent them from falling on the heads of passersby, a task he completed diligently. But the same period that mutilated the cathedral, well before the French Revolution, was also the one that rediscovered its architecture with the appearance of the first studies and guidebooks, which contain many

1780

Baroque Transformations

interesting observations about the monument. It was also the moment when major restoration works were undertaken in consideration of the medieval building, which was respected: restorations remained faithful to its appearance, to the point of fooling the restorers of the following century! For instance, Germain Bouffrand, the architect who retrofitted the chapel of Cardinal de Noailles in the baroque style, was charged by the same prelate with the delicate mission of restoring the rose window of the south transept façade (of Pierre de Montreuil) and to remake the crossing vault, which had been a cause for concern since the sixteenth century **(fig. 9)**. He took up the south rose again in 1727, without altering the intricate design of petals that fan out at the edges with radially arranged arches. Boffrand also retained the double-curved trefoils and quatrefoils, which Viollet-le-Duc mistook for an invention of his predecessor. When Viollet-le-Duc remade the rose window, he removed these elements, inventing the rounded form of the polylobes. These contradicted the blind tracery of the neighboring elements, which have remained intact since the thirteenth century.

The same Boffrand, in charge of the general hospital from 1724, was charged with the reconstruction of the

9. The crossing vault was entirely reconstructed in the early eighteenth century, as evidenced by the cherubs placed at the four cardinal points.

Hôpital des Enfants-Trouvés located on the rue Neuve-Notre-Dame. The new building enabled the widening of the old medieval street (which Maurice de Sully wanted) at the same time that it doubled the depth of the plaza at the west end of the cathedral. Work began in 1746. In the architect's mind, a second building on the other side of the street was supposed to form a monumental pendant to the façade of Notre Dame. The construction of a new door to the cloister against the north tower of the façade, the shape of a triumphal arch and built on the site of Saint-Jean-le-Rond, demolished in 1748, was Boffrand's final intervention in the cathedral precinct. It constituted an important step in the isolation of Notre Dame before it was cleared more completely through the efforts of Baron Haussmann.

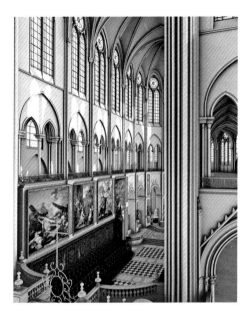

10 and 11. At left, on the ground level of a vessel made uniform by a layer of whitewash, the liturgical choir was transformed in the first half of the eighteenth century. Everything was renewed: pavement, choir stalls and altars, marble revetment and large oil paintings, a Baroque island within the Gothic church. At right, the state of the building in 2013.

But first, Notre Dame experienced the turbulence of the Revolution.

Paradoxically, the cathedral participated fully in the first phase of the Revolution. It was the backdrop for several key events of the new regime, and, in a certain sense, it helped legitimize them.

On November 10, 1793, the building was rededicated as a Temple of Reason. The Committee of Public Safety soon decreed that all of the painted and sculpted symbols of the Church and the monarchy had to be removed: Notre Dame should serve as an example. Toppled from their gallery, the kings broke into pieces as they fell onto the plaza below. The large jamb figures of the portals were destroyed. This work was not improvised; rather, it was part of a methodical campaign by paid workers acting on the orders of the contractor Varin. The debris remained on the ground for three years; it was eventually evacuated at the cost of rubble, above all as a hygienic measure, as the debris was being used as a urinal.

Varin was equally active inside the edifice. Everything that could be removed was either sold or transferred to the depot at the Petits-Augustins, the future Museum of French Monuments, which Alexandre Lenoir was establishing. The windows were broken; the majority of the altars and tombs were reduced to nothing; the bells were removed before being melted down, as was the majority of the sumptuous metalwork shrines and reliquaries. The building was used as a storehouse for all kinds of goods. For a time it was used to store works of art, and it was used to warehouse wine at the beginning of 1794. The cathedral crept toward the new century, humiliated like never before in a world that seemed to be coming to an end. ◆

This rendering presents the elevation and section of the cathedral
during the major restoration
undertaken by Jean-Baptiste
Lassus and Eugène-Emmanuel
Viollet-le-Duc. A comparison
to the renderings illustrating
the previous chapter reveals the
extent of the changes.

1860

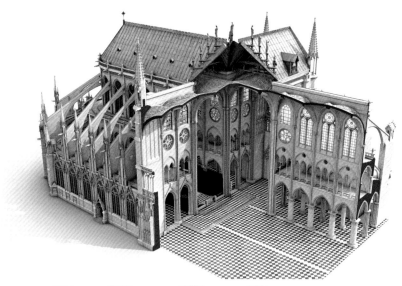

1860

The Major Restoration of Lassus and Viollet-le-Duc

Notre Dame in Peril

When the building was returned to the Church on April 18, 1802, the cathedral was in a pitiful state. In 1810, an official restoration campaign was launched under the direction of Alexandre-Théodore Brongniart. It was a heavy task: there had hardly been any funds allocated to the maintenance of the cathedral since the French Revolution. Brongniart died in 1813 without having had time to make his mark. Étienne-Hippolyte Godde, named architect of the city of Paris the same year, was designated as his successor despite his lack of experience in restoring medieval buildings. In 1820, Godde began by replacing eroded masonry with flagstones, following in the footsteps of Boulland. However, since

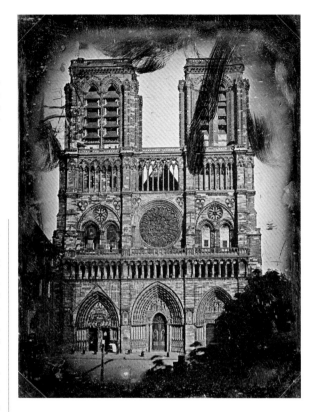

1. The chemical alteration of this daguerreotype of ca. 1840 by Fizeau seems to echo the disastrous state of conservation of the cathedral, which looks abandoned (Charenton-le-Pont, Médiathèque de l'Architecture et du Patrimoine).

this material was considered too heavy and problematic, he experimented with using mastic, a recent invention composed of linseed oil, lead oxide, and cement. It was an interesting idea, if not for the fact that linseed oil had a tendency to evaporate, causing the mastic to break down into powder. Godde undertook several other mediocre restoration projects. Critiques proliferated in increasing numbers at the ministry and among other observers.

It is still possible to see these interventions—later erased—in photographs, since they fortuitously coincided with the invention of that technology in France. Since the end of the 1830s, photographers including Hippolyte Bayard, Louis-Jacques-Mandé Daguerre, Armand-Hippolyte-Louis Fizeau, and Charles Nègre hastened to place their tripods in front of the west façade and the south flank of the building, recently exposed following the sack of the episcopal palace in 1831; they recorded changes made to the monument through daguerreotypes, calotypes, and glass negatives **(fig. 1)**. Their photographs are precious documents, visual evidence that allow us to consider the intentions of the different restoration architects.

The Invention of French Cultural Heritage

In the 1830s, at the very beginning of Louis-Philippe's reign, the emergence of an awareness of French cultural heritage as well as the rejection of negligence of all kinds began to crystalize, thanks to the efforts of a small group of tenacious and clever individuals. First among them was the historian and minister François Guizot, who did all he could to place the idea of cultural heritage

1860

The Major Restoration of Lassus and Viollet-le-Duc

at the heart of a new sense of national identity. Of all monuments, none surpassed the cathedral of Paris: as Baron Ferdinand de Guilhermy later wrote, "the history of Notre Dame is intimately linked to the entire history of France."

François-René de Chateaubriand (*The Genius of Christianity*), Charles de Montalembert (*Du vandalisme et du catholicisme dans l'art*), and Victor Hugo (*The Hunchback of Notre Dame*) were catalysts for this nascent interest in neglected buildings, and in the cathedral of Paris in particular. Others deserve to be cited, including Jean-Philippe Schmit, who worked in the French ministry of religious affairs until 1840; his volume *Les Églises gothiques*, published in 1837, introduced fundamental concepts in the ongoing debate surrounding restoration. Antiquarian groups would also enter the fray, thanks to the painstaking documentary work of figures like Arcisse de Caumont, Auguste Le Prévost, and Baron Justin Taylor (his *Voyages pittoresques et romantiques dans l'ancienne France* is the most well-known example).

Guizot wanted the government to get heavily involved in the protection of French cultural heritage. To that end, he created, in 1830, the position of Inspector General of Historic Monuments, tasked with compiling a list of buildings that needed protection and granting subventions for their maintenance. Guizot also founded, in 1837, the Committee on Arts and Monuments, whose members (Prosper Mérimée, Ludovic Vitet, Baron Taylor, Charles Lenormant, and Adolphe-Napoléon Didron, among others) were often mistaken for those of the Commission on Historic Monuments, created the same year. In fact, it was the Council on Civic Buildings, the oldest and the most powerful of these various government institutions capable of acting on behalf of historic monuments, that was granted the power to determine the fate of Notre Dame. In 1842, the council created a three-person committee that was charged with supervising a complete restoration: Mérimée (who was then inspector general of historic monuments), Charles Rohault de Fleury (inspector general of the council on civic buildings) and the architect Jacques-Félix Duban. This initiative was, in part, intended to respond to a petition that had circulated denouncing the building's poor state of preservation, signed by figures as illustrious as the archbishop of Paris, Hugo, Montalembert, and Didron and submitted to the minister of religious affairs, Pierre Dessauret.

2 and 3. North elevation of the nave: above, a hypothetical reconstruction of the state of the building before the restoration by Lassus and Viollet-le-Duc; below, a photograph of the post-restoration state of the building.

The Competition

Dessauret removed Godde (or else he quit—the archival documents are not clear on this point) and asked the architect Jean-Jacques Arveuf-Fransquin to submit a proposal for the restoration work. This decision attracted the attention of the architects Jean-Baptiste Lassus and Eugène-Emmanuel Viollet-le-Duc, who requested permission to submit a proposal as well. Their request was granted in October 1842, and it was thus that the idea of a competition began to take shape. A fourth architect, Jean-Charles Danjoy, was also authorized to participate. The candidates did not receive any written instructions; according to the terms of a report prepared later, there was a "complete lack of a plan for the restoration of the metropolitan church." The deadline was set for January 31, 1843, which left little time to prepare a proposal. Lassus and Viollet-le-Duc were the only ones to submit a project on time.

1860

The Major Restoration of Lassus and Viollet-le-Duc

On the recommendation of Mérimée, Rohault de Fleury, and Duban, on April 30, 1844, the Council on Civic Buildings named Lassus and Viollet-le-Duc "architects of the metropolis," whose mission was to develop an official plan for the restoration. In November of the same year, they were entrusted with the maintenance of the cathedral, at which point they boldly, and somewhat strategically, decided to shore up the flying buttress at the southwest corner of the choir, which was threatening collapse. It was more urgent than ever that the restoration work begin.

The Project

The *Projet de restauration de Notre-Dame de Paris* by Lassus and Viollet-le-Duc, submitted in January 1843 and published that same year, would have been music to the ears of the committee. The architects wrote,

> In such a project, we must act with the utmost prudence and discretion; and we will be the first to say that a restoration can be more disastrous for a monument than the ravages of time or popular vandalism! That is because time and revolutions destroy, but they do not add anything. But a restoration, to the contrary, adds new forms and removes many traces whose scarcity and state of ruin actually add to their interest. In this case, it is difficult to know which to fear more: the carelessness of letting fall to the ground that which threatens ruin, or the ignorant zeal that adds, recuts, completes, and finishes by transforming an old monument into a new monument, despoiled of all historical interest.

And yet other passages in the text clearly demonstrate that Lassus and Viollet-le-Duc had no intention of limiting themselves to preserving the building in its current state. This did not escape the attention of the Council on Civic Buildings—nor of César Daly, editor of the *Revue générale de l'architecture et des travaux publics*—even if the case of Notre Dame could only be exceptional, given its symbolic importance and its function as a cathedral. "An architect," wrote Lassus and Viollet-le-Duc in their *Projet*, "must make every effort to give back to the edifice, through prudent restorations, the richness and glow of which it has been deprived." And yet, Daly worried, "restoring the splendor of the edifice" did not mean to restore it but to complete it "following a fairly vague ideal."

Daly was particularly alarmed because of the past restorations realized by the two architects. The work of Lassus at Saint-Germain-l'Auxerrois was not without its detractors, and Viollet-le-Duc only had the restoration of the abbey church of Mary Magdalene of Vézelay

4. South flank, ca. 1855. The stones used by the restorers appear lighter than the ones in place before the restoration began.

under his belt. "If we must sacrifice a few monuments to instill in young architects an understanding of Gothic architecture," wrote Daly, "we would do well to have them care for monuments with the least artistic and historical value, but we should not teach them rhetoric and philosophy, that is, we should not be teaching them the basics, in a word, at the expense of the cathedral of Paris." Daly's critique was prescient. It was only later, when the public understood what the architects had in mind, that criticism was voiced more urgently.

Mérimée, Rohault de Fleury, and Duban specified that the restoration work should be divided into three categories: first of all, urgent work, including the replacement of "sick stones" and the repair of the center portal of the west façade. "The traces of mutilation," they wrote, "are so evident, or should we say, so shocking,

that it seems to us necessary to remove them." Next came the re-creation of different elements removed or altered, and, finally, the embellishment of the edifice. It was the second category that would turn out to be the most delicate. At the moment of creating their project, the architects did not yet have a deep understanding of the building, to the point that they had to modify their plans as they went along. Only financial considerations, with the tripling of the initial budget, constrained the extent of the interventions, which largely exceeded the original terms of the project. The neglect, revolutionary vandalism, and misguided restorations seem negligible by comparison to the work of Lassus and Viollet-le-Duc during the twenty-year restoration campaign. There is some truth to the aphorism that Notre Dame is largely a nineteenth-century building **(fig. 4)**.

1860
The Major Restoration of Lassus and Viollet-le-Duc

5. Center portal of the west façade. The lower lintel and the central portion of the upper lintel were re-created, repairing the damage Soufflot inflicted on the medieval sculpture.

The Restoration

Below are five examples of the changes Lassus and Viollet-le-Duc made to the cathedral.

The West Façade

The missing sculptures of the west façade, including the damaged ones of the center portal **(fig. 5)**, the embrasures, and the gallery of kings, as well as the crockets and gargoyles Parvy removed sixty years earlier, were made anew. While the work was inspired and its quality excellent, these changes exemplify the extent to which this was a modern reconstitution of the building. Lassus and Viollet-le-Duc emphasized its legitimacy on the grounds that the cathedral of Paris was a living monument. While it was feasible to preserve Gallo-Roman ruins as they were, Notre Dame, located at the heart of Paris and even of France itself, needed to remain functional and its sculptural program needed to be complete so that it could fulfill the mission of every cathedral: to address the faithful.

The Spire

In their project of 1843, Lassus and Viollet-le-Duc proposed to reconstruct the spire. Their plan, based on fairly extensive documentation concerning the original spire, was illustrated in an elevation drawing included in their project **(fig. 6)**. It is instructive to compare this drawing with the spire that was eventually realized **(fig. 7)**, redesigned by Viollet-le-Duc following the death of Lassus in 1857: it is a spectacular variation on the theme of a thirteenth-century spire, slimmer than the original, and with the significant addition of sculptures featuring the apostles distributed along the slope of the roof. Viollet-le-Duc appears among them in the guise of Saint Thomas, the patron saint of architects **(fig. 8)**.

8. Viollet-le-Duc as Saint Thomas; statue by Adolphe-Victor Geoffroy-Dechaume (1816–1892).

6. Elevation of the south flank by Lassus and Viollet-le-Duc included in the project of 1843, with a spire inspired by the one removed at the end of the eighteenth century (Charenton-le-Pont, Médiathèque de l'Architecture et du Patrimoine).

7. South flank of the cathedral in 2013.

1860

The Major Restoration of Lassus and Viollet-le-Duc

The Upper Windows of the Transept

In July 1854, as work progressed on the south side of the nave, fragments of oculi were discovered at the base of the thirteenth-century clerestory windows, embedded in the wall above the tribunes. It was an astonishing find: the original elevation of the Gothic building, still somewhat misunderstood at the time, was revealed. But the architects' response to this information amounted to one of the most controversial interventions they made to the fabric of the building. In August and September of the same year, three oculi were reconstructed in the last bay on the south side of the nave and in the two adjacent bays of the south transept arm; the high windows were restored in their twelfth-century state, based on the example of the first bay of the nave **(fig. 9)**. From June to September 1857, the operation was repeated on the north side. The insertion of new oculi involved the destruction, pure and simple, of the thirteenth-century windows, a decision Viollet-le-Duc justified on the grounds that the structural reinforcement was necessary to bear the load of the projected spire **(figs. 2–3)**. From February to July 1858, the operation was repeated in the choir, where the archaeological evidence was more tenuous.

The original oculi had been placed under the roofs above the tribune vaults; since these roofs were suppressed when the clerestory windows were enlarged in the thirteenth century, the new oculi were exposed to the elements **(fig. 10)**. Therefore, Lassus and Viollet-le-Duc logically decided to glaze them. This made an already controversial reworking even less defensible, since it profoundly altered the appearance of the third story of the elevation.

9. West wall of the south transept arm and north wall of the nave. The oculi inserted by Viollet-le-Duc no longer open onto the space under the roof but are instead glazed.

10. Southwest corner of the choir: redone clerestory and oculus. The billet moldings of the archivolt and the colonnettes are original, as are those of the adjacent bay.

1860

The Major Restoration of Lassus and Viollet-le-Duc

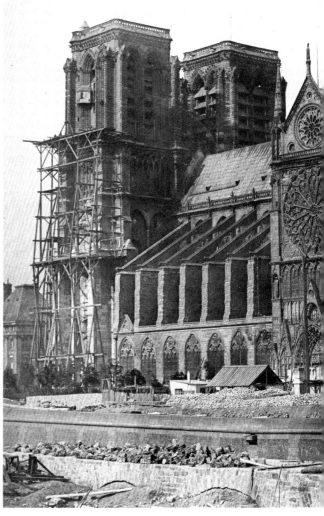

11. South flank of the cathedral, by Bayard, 1846 (Collection Société française de photographie). The south transept rose and the nave buttresses had not yet been modified; the choir buttresses are in the process of being redone.

The South Transept Rose Window

Germain Boffrand had already reworked the rose window of the south transept façade in 1725 at the behest of Cardinal de Noailles. However, Boffrand did not adequately consolidate the impost above the opening, as the photographs taken in the 1840s show **(fig. 11)**. In addition, according to Viollet-le-Duc, its execution and the materials used were of poor quality. Therefore, Lassus and Viollet-le-Duc dismantled the rose window to repair the impost and insert an iron tie to prevent the transept buttresses from moving. The rose window was reconstituted with more robust, reconfigured tracery, not as it had been but rotated by a half petal, in an almost obsessive gesture, so that the tracery would support the impost more directly **(fig. 12)**.

12. The south rose window as it was in 2013, rotated a half-petal.

The Flying Buttresses

The flying buttresses of the choir were entirely reworked between August 1846 and July 1858 **(figs. 11 and 13)**, an intervention apparently only partially necessitated by structural flaws. In his writing on the subject, Viollet-le-Duc highlighted his veritable revulsion toward the modern work undertaken at the cathedral before his nomination, to the point that he wanted to take it down at all costs. The fourteenth-century uprights of the flying

1860

The Major Restoration of Lassus and Viollet-le-Duc

buttresses, partly encased in heavy masses of masonry—probably added in the eighteenth century—were sacrificed in favor of a new buttressing system. In the nave, the first formal modification made to the flying buttresses was inspired by a sixteenth-century text by Gilles Corrozet, and, as Lassus and Viollet-le-Duc wrote, by "the fragments in situ." It consisted of adding an aedicule to the summit of each upright **(fig. 14)**. However, the text did not specifically describe the nave flying buttresses, and the iconographic sources—to which the architects had access—did not show any aedicules or pinnacles on the uprights. The reference to both textual and archaeological sources seems to have been a way to justify a questionable addition, intended to give the flying buttresses a form more in keeping with the established ideas they had about thirteenth-century architectural form.

The Rational Cathedral

Confronted with this series of archaeologically, iconographically, and theoretically problematic interventions, we are hard-pressed to find any justification for them besides an excess of hubris. Viollet-le-Duc did little to counter this impression. The introduction to the "Restoration" entry in his *Dictionnaire raisonnée* declares bluntly that "to restore an edifice means neither to maintain it, nor to repair it, nor to rebuild it; it means to reestablish it in a finished state, which may in fact never have actually existed at any given time."

Viollet-le-Duc was versed in the language and methods of the natural sciences, in the vein of Georges Cuvier: "The monuments of the Middle Ages," he wrote, "are cleverly calculated, their organism is fragile. There is nothing excessive in them, nothing useless; if you were to change one part of the organism, you would have to modify the rest." If the cathedral was an organism, then Viollet-le-Duc placed it on the examination table in order to dissect it with the scalpel of an all-encompassing and explicit idea; during the course

13. The flying buttresses of the south flank of the choir.

14. The flying buttresses of the south flank of the nave, with the tabernacles added by Lassus and Viollet-le-Duc (see figure 11 for the pre-restoration state).

of the operation, he was able not only to diagnose its different pathologies, structural and otherwise (introduced in large part during the preceding centuries), but also to discern—as one would for a living and breathing organism—its underlying reasoning. "The artist," wrote Lassus and Viollet-le-Duc in their *Projet*, "must disappear entirely . . . in order to locate and follow the reasoning that gave shape to the work he wishes to restore." Overseeing the fertile laboratory that was the building site, Lassus and Viollet-le-Duc persuaded themselves that they had located the original essence of the building, partially masked by later additions. Having the strength of their convictions, and from their privileged position as chief architects, they permitted themselves to rework the edifice in the service of historical, structural, visual, and functional unity previously unknown at the cathedral. ◆

The Cathedral Today

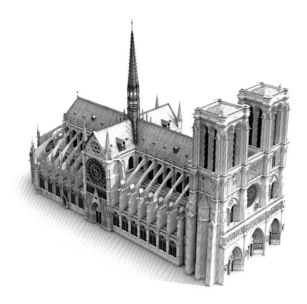

The Cathedral Today

The large-scale restoration work led by Lassus and Viollet-le-Duc now forms part of the monument. It represents a page in the building's history, to the extent that the idea emerged that Notre Dame is an entirely nineteenth-century monument. The popularity of certain additions has contributed to this myth: gargoyles and monstrous figures populating the upper reaches of the cathedral attest to this period that interpreted the medieval imaginary in an extremely creative way. While the structure of Notre Dame remains fundamentally an edifice of the twelfth and thirteenth centuries, it is also the case that the remaking in the nineteenth century of its most delicate elements—tracery of the clerestory and rose windows, flying buttresses, monumental sculpture—radically transformed its appearance, like Haussmannian Paris itself.

The restorations undertaken at the monument since Viollet-le-Duc were more modest, but they were undergirded by the principle that Notre Dame was aging inexorably and that the work of nineteenth-century

1. In the Porte Rouge, the first voussoir at left is a recent copy of a ruined sculpture put in place by Viollet-le-Duc. The other reliefs date to the thirteenth century.

2. The new high altar is now placed in the crossing for greater visibility.

architects required as much attention and care as the medieval elements. The recent recreation of a voussoir created by Viollet-le-Duc to replace a damaged element of the Porte Rouge was thus undertaken in keeping with the work of the nineteenth-century sculptors **(fig. 1)**.

The recent major cleanings of the building have been the most substantial. Following a first campaign in the late 1960s (under Minister of Culture André Malraux), the restoration of the western frontispiece was finished in time for the new millennium. It revealed details in the sculptural program long obscured by a thin layer of dirt visible in postwar photographs. The industrial age has accelerated the alteration of the masonry, but the phenomenon is not new. An inscription still legible in the seventeenth century, located near the statues decorating the outer wall of the choir chapels, evoked a cleaning dating to 1326:

Nos cottes crottées décrottées furent
Et nos faces trop mieulx en durent
M CCC XXVI

The situation has certainly gotten worse over the course of the past two centuries, necessitating constant maintenance of the superstructure.

The liturgical furnishings, radically reformed after the Second Vatican Council (1963–65), have undergone the most significant changes since the nineteenth century. A new high altar, created in 1989 by Jean and Sébastien Touret, was installed in the crossing **(fig. 2)**; it was enhanced by the creation of a new podium, realized in 2004 by Jean-Marie Duthilleul. Another example is the cross dominating the *Pietà* by Nicolas Coustou at the end of the apse: the artist Marc Couturier redid it in

The Cathedral Today

1994. Open for even longer to contemporary creations, the glass of Notre Dame was completely reworked. Only the three rose windows contain elements of medieval glass; the choir, for its part, retains its nineteenth-century neo-Gothic glass. In the second half of the twentieth century, to these were added panels of abstract glass featuring primary colors—above all blue and red—designed by Jacques Le Chevallier. They emphasize the architectural coherence and sobriety of the nave **(fig. 3)**.

Until quite recently, the period of significant transformations to the cathedral seemed to have been put firmly in the past, and we came to appreciate the extent of the dramatic human interventions throughout the cathedral's history, which left it without most of its surrounding buildings, isolated from the city at the end of an oversized plaza. Yet archaeological evidence sometimes reveals new information about the function of the episcopal group: for example, the urbanism effort of the early 1970s that focused on the plaza in front of the cathedral enabled the excavation of an area around Notre Dame, including the infrastructure of the houses lining rue Neuve-Notre-Dame—which Maurice de Sully had had constructed to lead directly to the new Gothic cathedral **(fig. 4)**. A clear line in the modern pavement indicates the outline of urban fabric no longer visible above ground **(fig. 8)**, clearer traces of which remain in the archaeological crypt located under the northern half of the plaza.

4. The plaza of Notre Dame in the process of being excavated, 1970 (Commission du Vieux Paris).

5. Remarkable discovery in 1977 of heads and other sculptural fragments from Notre Dame (Commission du Vieux Paris).

There have also been captivating art-historical discoveries concerning Notre Dame, such as the 1977 discovery of a veritable cemetery of medieval sculptures originating from the cathedral. During work in the basements of a bank located on the rue de la Chaussée-d'Antin, twenty-one of the twenty-eight heads of the colossal statues from the gallery of kings were exhumed from the courtyard of the former residence of Jean-Baptiste Lakanal. The royalist (not to be confused with his brother Joseph, who voted to put Louis XVI to death) had recovered these fragments—whose fate remained a secret—and saw to it that they received a proper burial **(fig. 5)**. They are now on public view at the Musée de Cluny. With other vestiges found since the nineteenth century, these heads form an impressive panorama of Gothic sculpture of the twelfth and thirteenth centuries, of which Notre Dame (along with Chartres and Reims Cathedrals) offers the widest range.

The Cathedral Today

6. Fragment of the painted decoration outside a choir chapel representing a funeral procession, fourteenth century (cathedral treasury).

Study of the monument itself has allowed for countless discoveries on the basis of traces of polychromy: they indicate that the sculptures and the principal members of the architecture were painted, which changes our perception of the cathedral considerably. There is no need to risk life and limb to detect them. Despite its degraded state, a displayed fragment of the painted decoration originating from the exterior of the radiating chapels in the current treasury of Notre Dame says a great deal about the ornamental richness of the cathedral since the Middle Ages **(fig. 6)**. Who now notices the blessing Christ, on the verso of the portal of the south transept arm, hidden under a layer of dust, that resembles the large Christ of the Last Judgment of the center portal of the west façade **(fig. 7)**? The cathedral contains many works that remain relatively unknown.

While it only possesses fragments of its medieval relic treasury, in 1806 Notre Dame received, in a great historical irony, the Crown of Thorns. Until the French Revolution, this relic had been kept in the Sainte-Chapelle on the Île de la Cité, which, in the mid-thirteenth century, had robbed the cathedral of its status as the capital's primary relic sanctuary. To offer greater solemnity to the building, the plaza in front of the cathedral was substantially enlarged in the nineteenth century **(fig. 8)**. Between the new Hôtel-Dieu built during the Second Empire, the police prefecture, and the Seine, it offers the cathedral a disembodied place detached from an urban context judged too haphazard for a monument built as a national icon. In front of the cathedral, on this plaza, a plaque marks the point from which distances in France are measured.

Less affected by the regime changes suffered by its rivals more closely associated with royal power, such as the Sainte-Chapelle and Saint-Denis, today Notre Dame alone may be seen as a kind of national sanctuary. In the tradition of the solemn ceremonies that occurred there even before its completion, the cathedral was frequently the site of state visits and funerals of heads of state. The bells of Notre Dame have tolled to mark important events in national history. The installation

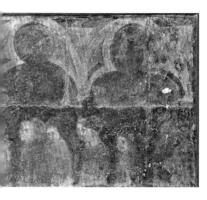

7. Blessing Christ placed atop the central gable on the verso of the south transept portal, ca. 1260.

8. The plaza viewed from the top of the west towers. The lighter stones in the pavement mark the contour of the medieval urban fabric, demonstrating how much larger the modern plaza is relative to past iterations.

of a new suspended bell on Easter 2013 gave even more of a voice to Notre Dame. The bells were silenced by the drama of the 2019 fire that destroyed the roof and the spire and threatened to destroy the entire edifice. The coming years will see a long restoration process, necessary to dress the cathedral's wounds. The general movement in favor of its repair recalls the popular fervor of the Middle Ages. This is yet another example of the historical continuity Notre Dame embodies. ◆

Conclusion

Notre Dame has long shown that it is a monument in constant dialogue with its time. The cathedral of the twelfth century was a pioneering building that surpassed in height all structures made by human hands since antiquity. Mastering stonemasonry, making the structure impossibly light, perfecting the buttressing, and creating rose windows larger and lighter than ever before placed this monument at the pinnacle of architectural innovation. Contemporaries were not wrong: Robert de Torigni, abbot of Mont-Saint-Michel and eyewitness to the construction in the late 1170s, declared that when it was finished, the cathedral would be unrivaled north of the Alps.

This propensity for experimentation would persist into the mid-thirteenth century, made possible by innovative architects. Their names come down to us: from Pierre de Montreuil to Raymond du Temple, they left us some of the best examples of the architecture we now call Rayonnant. This is visible in the circular, concentric forms of the transept roses and the increasingly delicate outlining of forms, as at the level of the new uprights of the flying buttresses of the choir.

The cathedral was also a stage for other intellectual feats, such as those undertaken by the clergy. Their intense theological reflections made a name for Paris even before the creation of the University of Paris in the thirteenth century. An unparalleled logic underpinned the composition of the west portals, particularly that of the Last Judgment (center) and the one glorifying the Virgin Mary, patron of the church (north); she was the reflection of the intellectual activity undertaken in the cathedral school from which emerged the leading theologians of the period. It was likely at Notre Dame that the rite of the elevation first took place: the celebrant priest elevated the chalice and host at the moment of the Eucharist, thereby demonstrating the mystery of transubstantiation to onlookers. The demands of the liturgy—to offer a place free from ambient noise in which to get close to the relics housed in the sanctuary—help explain the creation of a choir screen, composed of blind and openwork sections, surrounding the liturgical choir and the sanctuary that occupied the main vessel east of the transept. Notre Dame was likewise innovative in this respect, and the monumentality of these elements would be repeated into the late Middle Ages and beyond, as at Albi, Amiens, and Chartres. The development of the cult of the dead and the proliferation of votive masses became the impetus for the construction of chapels flanking the nave and, later, the choir, an approach that would be repeated frequently elsewhere in the centuries that followed.

We might be inclined to believe that the cathedral followed the principles of the Counter-Reformation, but the complete renovation of the liturgical choir with the installation of the sculptural ensemble depicting the Vow of Louis XIII—a new high altar at the back of the apse, between the statues of Louis XIII and Louis XIV—however late, was still imitated throughout the eighteenth century, with iron grilles replacing the stone screens to provide visual access to the sanctuary, retrofitted in a decidedly Baroque style. Long linked to the monarchy, Notre Dame paid a price for this connection, enduring assaults from revolutionary vandals who methodically suppressed any royal symbols found in its monumental sculptural program. Mutilated, the edifice had yet more to suffer in the absence of upkeep, which lasted until the 1830s.

With the awakening of consciousness of the importance of the monument for both the history of art and the history of France, a new era began, launched by the great restoration of Lassus and Viollet-le-Duc, which, despite the criticism it has endured, marks a high point in the formation of cultural heritage. This restoration, in many instances closer to a remaking, was so drastic that it seemed likely to put an end to the cathedral's monumental construction history, subsequently punctuated only by minor cleaning operations. But the catastrophe of April 15, 2019, suggests otherwise, as the timber framework, lead roof, and crossing spire were all destroyed. Now begins a new phase in the history of the edifice, which will require complex interventions to repair the extensive structural damage. The cathedral may have escaped total ruin, but the full extent of the damage remains to be assessed. A careful study of the monument—in which laser-scanning technology will play a role—will enable specialists to identify the problems, an indispensable step toward a thoughtful restoration. ◆

Plan of Notre Dame: Principal Phases of Construction

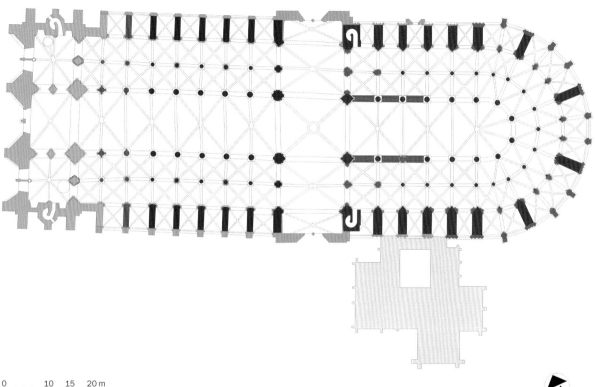

0   10   15   20 m

	ca. 1160–1182		ca. 1225–1270
	ca. 1180–1200		ca. 1290–1330
	ca. 1200–1210		after 1844
	ca. 1210–1220		

GLOSSARY

aisle: Lateral *vessel* of a church that is, by definition, lower than the central *vessel*.

ambulatory: Annular *vessel* extending from the *aisles* and surrounding the *apse* of a church.

apse: Termination of the main *vessel* of a church, which houses the sanctuary.

archivolt: *Molding* articulating an arch.

baptistery: The building, usually centrally planned, where the baptism ceremony occurs.

bay: Spatial unit created between two supports.

belfry: Wooden structure inside the tower of a church from which bells are suspended.

boss: *Keystone* placed at the center of a vault at the intersection of the ribs.

buttress: Structural member projecting from a wall and ensuring its equilibrium. In a church with *flying buttresses*, the buttress receives the thrusts transferred to the *upright* above it.

canon: Member of the cathedral *chapter* who assists the bishop, particularly during liturgical services in the *choir*.

capital: Sculpted top of a pier or column that serves as a base for an arch.

chaplaincy: Foundation for religious services conferred upon chaplains, priests serving altars for the celebration of masses; by extension, the income of the celebrant in charge of these services.

chapter: Assembly of cathedral *canons*: by metonymy, designates their meeting room.

chevet: East end of a church, which houses the sanctuary, *choir*, *ambulatory*, and radiating chapels.

choir: Space reserved for the clergy where most of the liturgy takes place, isolated by a screen from the rest of the church.

choir stall: Wooden seat in the *choir* of a church reserved for the clergy.

clerestory: The group of windows inserted at the top of the wall of the main *vessel*.

cloister: Courtyard lined with covered galleries leading to buildings for the collective use of the *chapter* and, by extension, the quarter in which the *canons* reside.

crossing: Space formed by the intersection of the main *vessel* and the *transept*.

embrasures: Oblique parts flanking the door of a portal, which may be adorned with monumental statues.

ex-voto: Material token of thanks for a wish granted.

flying buttress: Structural apparatus ensuring the transfer of the thrust of the vaults from the superstructure above the *aisle* to the buttress *upright*.

formwork: Wooden structure installed at the building site to assemble the stones of an arch, dismantled once the masonry is stabilized.

gable: Ornamental triangular form adorning a *bay*, a window, or a portal.

hemicycle: Semicircular part of the *apse*.

high altar: Main altar of a church.

***jubé*:** Masonry screen that isolates the *choir* from the *nave*.

keystone: Block of stone carved in the form of a wedge and placed at the apex of an arch.

lintel: Block of stone, sometimes sculpted, placed above a door.

molding: Profiles and proportions of the architectural articulation (bases, cornices, abaci).

nave: Front part of a church, accessible to the public, unlike the *choir*, reserved for the clergy.

oculus: Circular opening.

pinnacle: Pyramidal aedicule crowning architectural elements (*buttresses*, *uprights*, tabernacles).

pointed arches: Arches whose combination forms the diagonals of a Gothic vault.

shaft: Cylindrical, elongated part of a column or colonnette between the base and the *capital*.

shrine: Reliquary in the form of a chest with a sloped top containing the sacred remains, or relics, of a saint.

tracery: Network of stone subdividing a window opening.

transept: *Vessel* perpendicular to the main *vessel*, which forms the arms of a cross-shaped plan.

transverse arch: Arch of the vault, perpendicular to the wall and marking the *bay* divisions.

tribune: Gallery above an *aisle*.

trumeau: Sculpted pier supporting the *lintel* of a portal.

tympanum: Sculpted element in the form of a round or *pointed arch*, placed above the *lintel* of a portal and under the *archivolts*.

upright: Vertical projection of a *buttress* from which a *flying buttress* springs.

vault cell: One quarter of a rib vault.

vault rib: Projecting element that forms the profile of the arches of a rib vault.

vessel: Space contained between two parallel longitudinal walls.

voussoirs: Sculpted or molded blocks whose combination forms an *archivolt*.

western frontispiece: Imposing multilevel structure at the west end of the church.

SELECTED BIBLIOGRAPHY

Albrecht, Stephan. "Le portail Saint-Étienne de la cathédrale de Meaux et son prototype parisien: Un 'copier-coller.'" *Bulletin monumental* 175, no. 1 (2017): 3–20.

Aubert, Marcel. *Notre-Dame de Paris: Sa place dans l'histoire de l'architecture du XIIᵉ au XIVᵉ siècle*. Paris: H. Laurens, 1920.

Auzas, Pierre-Marie, ed. *Actes du colloque international Viollet-le-Duc, Paris 1980*. Paris: Nouvelles Éditions Latines, 1982.

Baldwin, John W. *Paris, 1200*. Stanford: Stanford University Press, 2010.

Barbier, Josiane, Didier Busson, and Véronique Soulay. "Avant la cathédrale gothique." In Vingt-Trois et al., *Notre-Dame de Paris*, 17–28.

Baridon, Laurent. *L'imaginaire scientifique de Viollet-le-Duc*. Paris: Harmattan, 1996.

Bercé, Françoise, et al. "Dossier Notre-Dame de Paris." In *Monumental*, edited by Françoise Bercé and Claude Eveno, 8–87. Paris: Centre des monuments nationaux, 2000.

Blanc, Annie, Lise Leroux, Jannie Mayer, and Elisabeth Pillet. "Les grandes restaurations." In Vingt-Trois et al., *Notre-Dame de Paris*, 135–44.

Blanc, Annie, and Claude Lorenz. "Observations sur la nature des matériaux de la cathédrale Notre-Dame de Paris." *Gesta* 29 (1990): 132–38.

Bony, Jean. *French Gothic Architecture of the 12th and 13th Centuries*. Berkeley: University of California Press, 1983.

Branner, Robert. "Paris and the Origins of Rayonnant Gothic Architecture Down to 1240." *Art Bulletin* 44 (1962): 39–51.

———. *Saint Louis and the Court Style in Gothic Architecture*. London: Zwemmer, 1965.

Bruzelius, Caroline. "The Construction of Notre-Dame in Paris." *Art Bulletin* 69 (1987): 540–69.

Cahn, Walter. "The Tympanum of the Portal of Saint-Anne at Notre-Dame de Paris and the Iconography of the Division of the Powers in the Early Middle Ages." *Journal of the Warburg and Courtauld Institutes* 32 (1969): 55–72.

Camille, Michael. *The Gargoyles of Notre-Dame: Medievalism and the Monsters of Modernity*. Chicago: University of Chicago Press, 2009.

Clark, William, and Robert Mark. "Le chevet et la nef de Notre-Dame de Paris: Une comparaison entre les premières élévations." *Journal d'histoire de l'architecture* 2 (1989): 69–88.

Colombier, Pierre du. *Les chantiers des cathédrales: Ouvriers, architectes, sculpteurs*. Paris: Picard, 1973.

———. *Notre-Dame de Paris: Mémorial de la France*. Paris: Plon, 1966.

Daly, César. "Restauration projetée de Notre-Dame de Paris." *Revue générale de l'architecture et des travaux publics* 4 (1843): 137–41.

Davis, Michael T. "Splendor and Peril: The Cathedral of Paris, 1290–1350." *Art Bulletin* 80 (1998): 34–66.

Erlande-Brandenburg, Alain. *Notre-Dame de Paris*. Paris: Éditions de La Martinière, 1997.

Erlande-Brandenburg, Alain, Michel Fleury, and François Giscard d'Estaing. *Les rois retrouvés*. Paris: J. Cuénot, 1977.

Erlande-Brandenburg, Alain, Jean-Michel Leniaud, François Loyer, and Christian Michel, eds. *Autour de Notre-Dame*. Paris: Action artistique de la ville de Paris: 2003.

Erlande-Brandenburg, Alain, and Dominique Thibaudat. *Les sculptures de Notre-Dame de Paris au musée de Cluny*. Paris: Éditions de la Réunion des musées nationaux, 1982.

Farcy, René. "Les travaux de Soufflot à Notre-Dame." *La cité*, no. 114 (1930): 130–43.

Fleury, Michel. "Découvertes à Notre-Dame de Paris." *Archéologia* 183 (October 1983): 14–15.

Fonquernie, Bernard, Françoise Gatouillat, Benjamin Mouton, and Marc Vire. "Les matériaux mis en œuvre." In Vingt-Trois et al., *Notre-Dame de Paris*, 47–66.

Gady, Alexandre. "La cathédrale du roi." In Vingt-Trois et al., *Notre-Dame de Paris*, 117–26.

Gauvard, Claude, and Joël Laiter. *Notre-Dame de Paris: Cathédrale médiévale*. Paris: Éditions du Chêne, 2006.

Giraud, Cédric, ed. *Notre-Dame de Paris 1163–2013: Actes du colloque scientifique tenu au Collège des Bernardins à Paris, du 12 au 15 décembre 2012*. Turnhout: Brepols, 2013.

Guilhermy, Ferdinand de, and Eugène-Emmanuel Viollet-le-Duc. *Description de Notre-Dame, cathédrale de Paris*. Paris: B. Bance, 1856.

Hamon, Étienne. "Les abords de Notre-Dame au Moyen Âge." In Vingt-Trois et al., *Notre-Dame de Paris*, 109–16.

Hardy, Chantal. "Les roses dans l'élévation de Notre-Dame de Paris." *Bulletin monumental* 149, no. 2 (1991): 153–99.

Hayot, Denis. *Paris en 1200: Histoire et archéologie d'une capitale fortifiée par Philippe Auguste*. Paris: CNRS Éditions, 2018.

Huitième centenaire de Notre-Dame de Paris (congrès des 30 mai–3 juin 1964): Recueil de travaux sur l'histoire de la cathédrale et de l'église de Paris. Bibliothèque de la Société d'histoire ecclésiastique de la France. Paris: J. Vrin, 1967.

Joubert, Fabienne. *La sculpture gothique en France XIIe–XIIIe siècles*. Paris: Picard, 2008.

Kimpel, Dieter. *Die Querhausarme von Notre-Dame zu Paris und ihre Skulpturen*. Bonn: Rheinische Friedrich-Wilhelms-Universität, 1971.

Kimpel, Dieter, and Robert Suckale. *L'architecture gothique en France, 1130–1270*. Paris: Flammarion, 1990.

Kraus, Henry. *Gold Was the Mortar: The Economics of Cathedral Building*. London: Routledge and Kegan Paul, 1979.

Lassus, Jean-Baptiste, Maurice Ouradou, and Eugène-Emmanuel Viollet-le-Duc. *Monographie de Notre-Dame de Paris*. Paris: Morel, 1870. Reprint, Paris: Éditions Molière, 2008.

Lassus, Jean-Baptiste, and Eugène-Emmanuel Viollet-le-Duc. *Projet de restauration de Notre-Dame de Paris: Rapport adressé à M. le ministre de la Justice et des cultes, annexé au projet de restauration, remis le 31 janvier 1843*. Paris: Imprimerie de Mme de Lacombe, 1843.

Le Goff, Jacques. "Culture ecclésiastique et culture folklorique au Moyen Âge: Saint Marcel de Paris et le dragon." In *Richerche storiche ed economiche in memoria di Corrado Barbagallo*, edited by L. De Rosa, 2:51–90. Naples: Edizioni Scientifiche Italiane, 1970. Reprinted in Jacques Le Goff, *Un autre Moyen Âge* (Paris: Gallimard, 1999), 229–67.

Lheure, Michel. *Le rayonnement de Notre-Dame de Paris dans ses paroisses, 1170–1300*. Paris: Picard, 2010.

Lorentz, Philippe, and Dany Sandron. *Atlas de Paris au Moyen Âge: Espace urbain, habitat, société, religion, lieux de pouvoir*. Paris: Parigramme, 2006. Reprint, 2018.

Macé de Lépinay, François. "La restauration de la sculpture de Notre-Dame." In *De plâtre et d'or: Geoffroy-Dechaume, sculpteur romantique de Viollet-le-Duc*, 157–71. L'Isle-Adam: Val-d'Oise Éditions, 2000.

Mayer, Jannie. "Les premiers travaux de Lassus et Viollet-le-Duc à Notre-Dame de Paris: La galerie des Rois et les niches des contreforts de la façade ouest, 1844–1846." *Bulletin monumental* 157, no. 4 (1999): 355–65.

Murray, Stephen. "Notre-Dame of Paris and the Anticipation of Gothic." *Art Bulletin* 80, no. 2 (1998): 229–53.

Pillet, Elisabeth. "Dans les tempêtes de l'histoire." In Vingt-Trois et al., *Notre-Dame de Paris*, 127–34.

Prache, Anne. "Un architecte du XIIIᵉ siècle et son œuvre: Pierre de Montreuil." *Dossiers d'archéologie* 47 (November 1980): 26–39.

Reiff, Daniel. "Viollet-le-Duc and Historic Restoration: The West Portals of Notre-Dame." *Journal of the Society of Architectural Historians* 30 (1971): 17–30.

Salet, Francis. "Notre-Dame de Paris: État présent de la recherche." *La sauvegarde de l'Art français* 2 (1982): 89–113.

Sandron, Dany. "L'autre métamorphose de Notre-Dame de Paris: La réfection du décor d'orfèvrerie du sanctuaire (vers 1260–1340)." In *Mélanges en l'honneur de Klara Benesovska*, edited by Jan Chlibec and Zoë Opacic, 378–86. Prague: Artefactum, 2015.

———. "La cathédrale et les rois: Notre-Dame de Paris (XIIᵉ–XIIᵉ siècles)." In *Kirche als Baustelle: Grosse Sakralbauten des Mittelalters*, edited by Katja Schröck, Bruno Klein, and Stefan Bürger, 260–70. Cologne: Böhlau Verlag, 2013.

———. "La galerie des Rois de Notre-Dame de Paris." *Commission du Vieux-Paris, procès-verbaux* 5, no. 2 (May 2002): 10–15.

———. "La maîtrise d'œuvre." In Vingt-Trois et al., *Notre-Dame de Paris*, 40–45.

———. "Le projet du XIIᵉ siècle." In Vingt-Trois et al., *Notre-Dame de Paris*, 67–93.

———. "Les rois s'invitent à Notre-Dame." In *Les portails sculptés à la lumière de l'archéologie: Journée d'études Sculpture monumentale et archéologie, Université d'Amiens, 19 janvier 2009*, edited by Iliana Kasarska, 11–28. Paris: Picard, 2011.

———. "Une savante mise en scène des reliques: L'architecture et le décor monumental de Notre-Dame de Paris dans la seconde moitié du XIIIᵉ siècle." In *Cathédrale et pèlerinage aux époques médiévale et moderne*, edited by Catherine Vincent and Jacques Pycke, 89–103. Bibliothèque de la revue d'histoire ecclésiastique. Louvain-la-Neuve: Bibliothèque de la RHE, 2010.

Sandron, Dany, and Sabine Berger. "La maîtrise d'ouvrage." In Vingt-Trois et al., *Notre-Dame de Paris*, 29–37.

———. "Des transformations radicales." In Vingt-Trois et al., *Notre-Dame de Paris*, 94–100.

Tallon, Andrew. "Archéologie spatiale: Le bâtiment gothique relevé (et révélé) par laser." In *Architecture et sculpture gothiques: Renouvellement des méthodes et des regards*, edited by Arnaud Timbert and Stéphanie Daussy, 63–75. Art et Société. Rennes: Presses Universitaires de Rennes, 2012.

———. "An Architecture of Perfection." *Journal of the Society of Architectural Historians* 73, no. 4 (2013): 530–54.

———. "La technologie 3D au service de Notre-Dame." In Vingt-Trois et al., *Notre-Dame de Paris*, 158–60.

Taralon, Jean. "Observations sur le portail central et sur la façade occidentale de Notre-Dame de Paris." *Bulletin monumental* 149 (1991): 341–413.

Thirion, Jacques. "Les plus anciennes sculptures de Notre-Dame de Paris." *Comptes rendus de l'Académie des inscriptions et belles-lettres* 114, no. 1 (1970): 85–112.

Vingt-Trois, Cardinal André, Mgr Patrick Jacquin, Dany Sandron, Jean-Pierre Cartier, and Gérard Pelletier, eds. *Notre-Dame de Paris. La grâce d'une cathédrale*. Strasbourg: La Nuée Bleue, 2012.

Viollet-le-Duc, Eugène-Emmanuel. *Dictionnaire raisonné de l'architecture française du XIᵉ au XVIᵉ siècle*. Paris: B. Bance and A. Morel, 1854–68.

———. "Entretien et restauration des cathédrales de France: Notre-Dame de Paris." *Revue générale de l'architecture et des travaux publics* 9 (1851): 3–17.

Viollet-le-Duc, Geneviève. "La flèche de Notre-Dame de Paris." *Les monuments historiques de la France* 11 (1965): 43–50.

———. "Restauration de Notre-Dame de Paris: Découverte par Viollet-le-Duc des roses des travées de la nef." *Les monuments historiques de la France* 14 (1968): 108–9.

Wright, Craig M. *Music and Ceremony at Notre Dame of Paris, 500–1550*. Cambridge Studies in Music. Cambridge: Cambridge University Press, 1989.

Credits

Photographs of Notre Dame Cathedral are © Andrew Tallon, except where stated otherwise.